An Immigrant Story

An Immigrant Story

KENNETH E. BURCHETT

Amity America, Publishers
Branson, Missouri

Library of Congress Control Number: 2019909772

ISBN: 978-1-7333006-9-8 (hardcover)
ISBN: 978-1-7333006-0-5 (paperback)
ISBN: 978-1-7333006-3-6 (ebook)

On the cover: Wood engraving of
Emigrants at Dinner, 1847 (Illustrated London News)

Amity America, Publishers
One Seventeen Westwood Drive,
Branson, Missouri 65616

For Arthur

Contents

Preface

When I undertook to write this book, I knew something of the life of Henry and Margarethe Schaumann, mostly from their grandson, Arthur Schaumann, who happened to be my father-in-law. He told me how Henry had joined the Union army in the Civil War, had been with Sigel, and was hurt when his horse fell during maneuvers, causing a serious injury that ended his military career and eventually caused his death. He told me, too, of the long struggle Margarethe had with the US government to claim a widow's Civil War pension. I was enthralled by these stories, but it was not until I obtained a copy of the proceedings from the National Archives and Records Administration in Washington, D.C., that I understood all of what happened.

Part one of this book is about the life and times of Henry Schaumann. His life is reconstructed in the following pages from surviving documents. It is impossible to prove in every case the accuracy of the records. In Germany, the Schaumann name has many related spellings, and documents in America frequently use different spellings of the name for the same person. Enough points of congruence match in the various records of Henry's life and death, however, to write with a high degree of genealogical certainty a reliable account of his experiences.

Part 2 is an annotated chronology of Henry Schaumann's Civil War Pension Case. It includes transcribed documents produced by both Henry and his widow Margarethe.

Margarethe Ficke Schaumann has a genealogy that is accessible, especially covering her life in Missouri. Where no personal memory of Henry existed among his descendants, "Grandma Edelmann," as Margarethe was known in her later years, left fond memories recalling her sometimes difficult and full life.

Arthur was generally correct in what he remembered about his grandparents. The purpose of this book, then, is to fill in the details. Arthur did not live to see the outcome. The book is dedicated to his memory.

Life and Times of Henry Schaumann

1

Introduction

Over the course of four decades until his death in 1866, Henry Schaumann was a laborer, craftsman, mechanic, and house wright, a person who built and repaired houses. He knew life as a husband, father, and citizen at different times in two countries.

The proud tradition of his German heritage begins with his name. Heinrich (Henry in English) is an early Saxon name, dating at least to Henry I, or Henry the Fowler who lived from 876 to 936, the precursor of the Saxon line of German kings and emperors. It was under Henry I that the new realm of Germany was founded. A succession of Henrys ruled Germany off and on until 1313. The name continued in countless generations. Consequently, Heinrich is a common name in German and German American heritage.

There are no known photographs or personal mementoes of Henry Schaumann. The closest thing to a personal remembrance of his life is his signature on his Civil War pension application of 1863.

Of temperate disposition, he was of average height for the time, standing 5 feet 6½ inches tall, with dark complexion, grey eyes, and dark hair.[1] Little is known of his youth, except that he was born in Hildesheim, Germany, and spent time at Clauen, near Peine, a small village not far from Hildesheim. Like anyone, his life was no doubt deeply influenced by where he grew up.

He left his native country to become part of the melting pot of immigrant America. Facing a difficult and uncertain future in war-torn Germany, Henry joined tens of thousands of his fellow countrymen as they made their way to the ports of Europe in a new wave of migration. Departures of large numbers of young professionals and workers in the last half of the 19th Century

seriously depleted the work force of Germany and added
significantly to the growth and development of the United States,
particularly in regions of the Midwest. The traditions and values
they carried with them helped to shape the landscape of 19th
Century America.

Henry could not have known that the perils of war in
Germany would reappear in his life in the form of the American
Civil War.

2

The Kingdom of Hanover

The ancestral home of the Schaumann family was the land known historically as the Kingdom of Hanover, now Lower Saxony, Germany. It was from this place that Henry Schaumann began his journey to America.

The history of the Kingdom of Hanover (spelled Hannover in German), for which the present province of Hanover is named, goes back to the early Middle Ages. It began as a small rural settlement called Angila on the high banks of the River Leine at the crossing of two important ancient trading routes in what was known as the land of Saxony. Angila became a thriving community of traders and craftsmen, was renamed Hanover, and for centuries it prospered as a well-fortified city.

The Thirty Years War, a series of territorial, political, and religious wars that lasted from 1618 to 1648, dramatically changed Europe and the course of European history. The Thirty Years War was a widespread war fought mainly in Germany between German Catholics and German Protestants. The general result of the war was a significant decrease in German population, devastation of German agriculture, and ruin of German commerce and industry. It effectively broke up what remained of the Holy Roman Empire and spelled the end of the greatness of the Hapsburgs—the ruling house of Austria, resulting in new power bases and alliances throughout Europe. Despite a treaty that ended the broad conflict, hostilities continued for decades among various parties, especially the Germans and French. In 1692, as a reward for service against the French, the Protestant Duke of Hanover, Ernest Augustus, was made an Elector of all territory encompassing the city of Hanover and surrounding lands. He called his little Electorate Hanover after its principal city.[1]

Little changed in the life of the people of Hanover until the 17th Century when, after decades of war and turmoil, the House of Hanover ascended to the throne of England.

Hanover's ties to Great Britain began in 1658 when Ernest Augustus married Sophia, the daughter of Elizabeth and granddaughter of James I of Great Britain. The British Act of Settlement in 1701 gave Sophia the right to succeed Queen Anne of England expressly because Sophia was Protestant and because neither Queen Anne nor her brother William produced heirs to the throne. However, Sophia died a few weeks before Queen Anne and so it was Sophia's son, Georg Ludwig (George Louis in English)—great grandson of James I—who in 1714 left Hanover to become George I, the first Hanoverian King of England. George, a German who did not speak a word of English, started the rule of the House of Hanover under which Britain achieved great wealth and peace over the next century.

George I married Sophia Dorothea, names incidentally common in Schaumann genealogy. George and Sophia had a daughter, also named Sophia Dorothea. Unfortunately, George I was an unpopular King due in part to his manners but due also to his treatment of Sophia Dorothea. She was divorced for her rumored infidelity—despite common knowledge of his own mistresses—and imprisoned. His son, George II, succeeded to the throne in 1727; his grandson, George III, began rule in 1760 as the first of the House of Hanover to be born in England. George III is remembered as the well-intentioned monarch whose bad judgment is credited with the loss of the American colonies and who witnessed the birth of the United States. George III ruled for fifty years.

Meanwhile, the Hanoverian King of England also continued to be the Elector of Hanover and, due to Hanover's connection with England, it was made a target of England's enemies. During the French Revolutionary Wars, for example, Hanover was occupied by the Prussians and the French, the latter until 1813. After the defeat of Napoleon in 1814, Hanover was raised to the position of the Kingdom of Hanover and made a member of the German Confederation.

Two decades later, the royal connection to England was severed. According to Hanoverian law, female succession to the rule of Hanover was only allowed if there were no male heirs. With the death of King William IV, King of England, in 1837, succession to the rule of the Kingdom of Hanover passed not to

William's niece, Victoria, who became queen of England, but to his brother, Ernest Augustus, the Duke of Cumberland and namesake of the first Hanoverian Elector.

Thus, Henry Schaumann was born a subject of Great Britain but relinquished that status when Ernest Augustus assumed power. Nevertheless, in 1826, the year in which Henry Schaumann was born, the King of England and the Elector of Hanover were still one and the same because George IV followed his father George III to the throne of England in 1820. An unpopular king, the rule of George IV lasted only ten years.

Upon the separation of Hanover from England with the crowning of Queen Victoria in 1837—when Henry Schaumann was eleven—the new King of Hanover, Ernest Augustus, immediately repealed the Hanover constitution.[2] The German Revolutions followed. The Revolution of 1848-1849, which happened concurrently in a number of European states, forced Ernest Augustus to reinstate a new liberal constitution for Hanover; but the lack of reconciliation of the several revolutions contributed greatly to the class antagonisms in Germany for succeeding decades.

The flags of Hanover were familiar to the Schaumann family and the rest of the world. As Hanover changed, so did its flag, as well as other symbols of its nationalism. The Hanover national anthem, for example, was heard not only in Hanover but also at coronations in England and later as a popular patriotic song in America. The anthem was created for George II and remained the national anthem of the United Kingdom after the end of the Hanover-England union in 1837. It is known today as "God Save the Queen." The music was adapted in 1832 by Samuel Francis Smith as "America My Country 'Tis of Thee" apparently without Smith knowing its origin. Other German states also made this melody their anthem. Its exact origin is unknown. Germans attributed it to Georg Friedrich Händel who was from Hanover and who served King George in London.

These were the times of Henry Schaumann in the Kingdom of Hanover. It is against this backdrop of events and history that he and thousands of German emigrants like him left their war-torn mother country for the uncertain promise of a better life in America.

His decision to leave Hanover for the United States was no doubt influenced by the unrest in Germany. When Ernest Augustus died in 1851, his son George V who had been blind since the age of fourteen succeeded him to the Hanover throne. During the power struggle between Prussia and Austria, George V tried to maintain a state of neutrality but fell into alliance with Austria and was defeated by the Prussian army. He was forced into exile, and on September 20, 1866, the Kingdom of Hanover was annexed by Prussia and made into the province of Hanover. No longer distinguished as a kingdom, it became a part of the German Empire in 1871, and in 1916, it was absorbed into the modern German state of Lower Saxony.

The boundaries of the province of the old Kingdom of Hanover are little changed from early times. A territory of about 15,000 square miles—about half the size of the state of Maine, it is bordered by The Netherlands and the North Sea on the northwest and by the Harz Mountains in the southeast. It remains a rich agricultural lowland situated between the Elbe and Weser Rivers.[3] Its old boundaries may be traced along the borders of the state of Lower Saxony; the lands of old Hanover make up most of present day Lower Saxony.

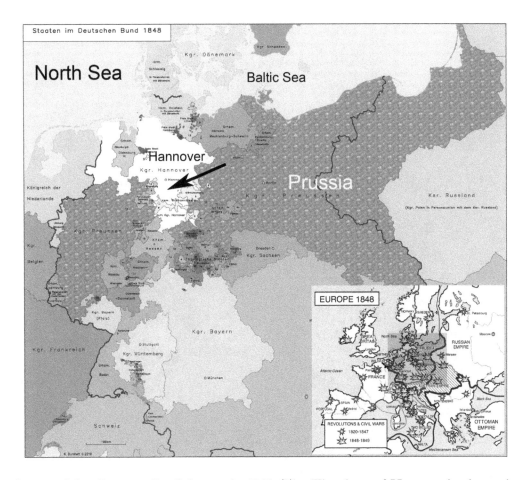

States of the German Confederacy in 1848. The Kingdom of Hanover is shown in white. An arrow marks the part of Hanover that was home to Henry Schaumann. The looming presence of Prussia (texture on the map) spreads over much of the region. Beginning about 1820, revolution and civil war spread across much of Europe. The map inset locates the centers of these uprisings and shows their proximity to Hanover. The unrest led to the German Revolution of 1848-1849, which caused many people to leave Germany and immigrate to America. Map by K. Burchett adapted from a map by A. Kunz & J.R. Moeschl, 2000; inset after B.A. Pavlac, 2000.

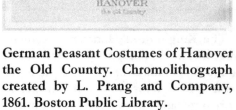

German Peasant Costumes of Hanover the Old Country. Chromolithograph created by L. Prang and Company, 1861. Boston Public Library.

King George IV. The unpopular King George IV was jointly the monarch of England and the Kingdom of Hanover when Henry Schaumann was born in Hanover. Lithograph from an original by G. Atkinson, Brighton, UK, 1821.

Burg Peine i. J. 1521.

Peine Castle War Scene. Troops under siege in the town of Peine, Germany, pictured in 1521 by an artist showing a scene from one of the many wars that rocked the country throughout its early history. Peine was at the center of the ancestral home of the Schaumann family. Lithograph, 6.5" x 9", c. 1850. Pinacotheca Brunsvicensis, Vol. 9, Duke August Library.

3

Birthplace of Henry Schaumann

Henry Schaumann was born in Hildesheim, Hanover, Germany, in 1826 at a time of exceptional political events in the region when the Kingdom of Hanover and the British Empire had the same king.[1] Growing up, Henry would have been familiar with the beauty of Hildesheim's natural setting, its fertile river land to the northwest, and its forested mountains to the south. The forested hill chains of the Hildesheim Forest and the Seven Mountains lie between the Leine and Innerste Rivers. Henry would have known, too, of the city's proud religious and cultural past.

When developing a genealogy of an immigrant ancestor, it is helpful to know something about his or her homeland. German geography has changed many times over the centuries. Fortunately, most German place names are the same today as they were historically; only boundaries have changed. Nevertheless, place names can be confusing. It is necessary, for instance, to know if a geographic reference is to a political place name or to one established by the dominant church; in this case, the Evangelical Lutheran National Church of Hanover. The borders of church districts were constantly changing and almost certainly were different in Henry's time in the 19th Century in the Hildesheim region.

Church districts did not always correspond to administrative districts, which were typically overseen by the district civil courts. German administrative districts were originally like states but today are more akin to US counties. Historically, a German district was commonly named after the major town or city within the district. Consequently, there was, and still is, a Hildesheim administrative district, a Hildesheim church region, and a Hildesheim church district, not to mention the city of Hildesheim itself.

Therefore, when Henry stated that he was born in Hildesheim several possibilities apply. He may have been referring to the city of Hildesheim, the church region, or district of that name, or to the administrative district of the same name, which at that time would have been called a state and not a district since it was a major political division of the Kingdom of Hanover. States were relegated to districts in 1866 when Prussia annexed Hanover.[2]

Hildesheim lies in the southeast corner of the state of Lower Saxony, at the base of the Harz Mountains of north Germany. Through it runs the Innerste River, a tributary of the Leine River that connects Hildesheim to the city of Hanover. Among the oldest cities in Europe, Hildesheim dates at least to the year 815 when Ludwig the Pious, son of Charlemagne, built a chapel there consecrated to the Virgin Mary amid the busy trade routes that characterized the Land of Saxony at that time. Thus began the city's history as an early medieval religious center of Christianity.[3]

After the era of Ludwig the Pious—and well before Henry Schaumann's time—Hildesheim grew up as an important outpost of the Roman Catholic Church, early on becoming a bishopric in the Church hierarchy. Under the Ottoman Empire, the city built some of the most beautiful examples of Romanesque and medieval architecture in the world, notably St. Mary's Cathedral and the Church of St. Michael, each dating to the 11th Century. One of Hildesheim's early bishops, Bishop Bernward, now Saint Bernward, is credited with the artistic legacy of Hildesheim. His interest in art and his determination to create the best works to be found outside of the Roman and Byzantine centers resulted by the year of his death in 1022 in examples of art and architecture that continue to be celebrated for their quality and uniqueness of style. The legendary 1,000-year-old rosebush of Hildesheim still climbs its way gracefully up the apse of the cathedral, a living symbol of the city's endurance.[4]

The craftsmen of Hildesheim are also said to have built the first half-timbered buildings, structures where the top floors extend cantilevered over the lower floors, a style that came to characterize much of German architecture. The world-famous market square, set amid the narrow, winding streets of old Hildesheim, features the Butchers' Guild House, built during the

Renaissance in 1529 and is among the best examples of half-timber construction.

The city of Hildesheim was chartered in 1249, and by 1460, the people of Hildesheim created a progressive democratic constitution, establishing the authority of the townspeople over that of the bishop's governor and effectively separating church and city government. One of the first newspapers in Germany appeared there in 1617, the first private theater was built in 1770, and in 1803 the city was secularized, and incorporated in 1815 into the Kingdom of Hanover where the fortunes of the Kingdom became those of the people of Hildesheim. Today, the city is an industrial and transportation center, protective of its cultural heritage, and well known for its progressive manufacturing and trade policies.[5]

The city was badly damaged at the end of World War II. Its citizens have since rebuilt it, taking great care to restore its architecture to its original splendor.

We do not know what personal relationships Henry Schaumann and his family had with the city of Hildesheim and the surrounding countryside. The city of Hildesheim would have been a place where he would have spent time in his youth before coming to the US; he would have known Hildesheim's cultural landmarks that are today major German heritage sites.

When Henry said he was born in Hildesheim, it is probable that he meant the larger state or region of Hildesheim and not the city of Hildesheim. Either way, it is correct to conclude that he was born in Hildesheim, Hanover, Germany, and grew to adulthood there. His last place of residence before immigrating to American was "Clauen, near Peine."[6]

A brief description of Peine and Clauen paints a different background experience from what one might encounter in a large city. The mining town of Peine lies northeast of the city of Hildesheim, being one corner of the Hildesheim-Hanover-Peine triangle, a small geographic region of about twenty miles on a side. Peine sets on the Fuhse River near the Mittleland Canal, a relatively modern water route that traverses east west through most of the southern length of the state of Lower Saxony.[7]

Peine dates from the 12th Century when an emissary of the emperor of the Holy Roman Empire built on the site Burg Peine, a castle outpost that is today the feature attraction of the city. A town grew up south of the castle beginning as early as 1223 when it gained town privileges in the hierarchy of German politics. Both the town and castle reverted to fiefdom briefly before being incorporated as a market town under Otto I, Bishop of Hildesheim.

Peine came to the attention of the world in 1963 when 29 miners died in a mine disaster. Eleven more miners were rescued after being trapped for two weeks. Once a mining and smelting town, the last existing steel works in Peine closed in 1976.[8]

Southwest of the city of Peine midway between Peine and Hildesheim sits the village of Clauen, a village and a church parish in the church district of Groß-Solschen bordering the Hildesheim church district on the south and the Peine church district to the north. Clauen lies between Hildesheim and Peine, distances of 7.5 and 8.1 miles respectively. When Henry said he was from Clauen, near Peine, he meant within a few miles.

In prehistoric times, Clauen was home to arable farmers and ranchers. First mentioned by name in historic records in 1151, the village has since the Protestant Reformation of 1542 hosted a congregation of the Evangelical Lutheran Church.

Home today to a population of about 1,000 residents, the village of Clauen was incorporated into the city of Hohenhameln in 1974, which at that time, in addition to Clauen, also took in nine other villages, making Clauen now part of a much larger metropolitan area than the small rural village that it was in Henry Schaumann's time.

Hildesheim St. Mary's Cathedral Cloisters with St. Anne's Chapel, in the time of Henry Schaumann. In the background, the Millennial Rose Tree is seen against the wall of the cathedral apse. Steel engraving by J. Poppel after a drawing by J.F. Long, c. 1845.

Butcher's Guild Hall, Hildesheim, Germany, Half-Timbered House. Built in 1529 and pictured as it appeared prior to World War II. The original structure was destroyed in 1945 by incendiary bombs and later reconstructed in the 1980s in its original 1529 style. Library of Congress.

1675 drawing of Peine Castle on the tip of the Old Town Peine Peninsula. The castle dates to the 12th Century, placing the city of Peine among the oldest cities in Germany. Courtesy of the District Home Association of Peine.

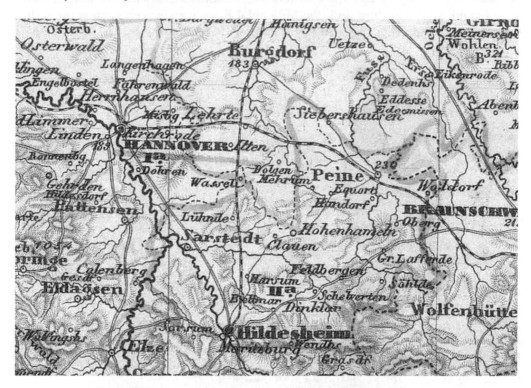

Hanover-Hildesheim-Peine Triangle. The village of Clauen is located between Hildesheim and Peine. From an engraved map of Hanover, 1851. J. Meyer, et al. *Grosser Hand-Atlas Uber Alle Theile Der Erde In 170 Karten*. Hildburghausen: Bibliographischen Instituts, 1860.

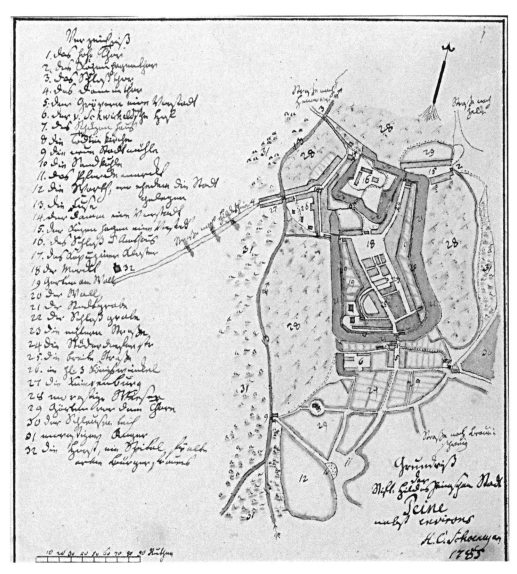

The Old Town Peninsula with the Peine Castle at the northwestern tip. Textured areas on the map show Old Town surrounded by bog on three sides. Drawing by H.C. Schoenejan, 1785. 5" x 4.7". Herzog Anton Ulrich Museum.

4

Journey to America

Henry Schaumann first set foot in America sometime before the year 1861, one of many young immigrants departing the declining circumstances in Germany for a more promising if uncertain future in the United States. He left Clauen for a distant shore far across the Atlantic Ocean.

There were many emigrant ships that sailed west in those days. Besides Germany, mass emigration out of Great Britain and Ireland took place on a grand scale. Famine and the threat of war drove people out by the hundreds of thousands. In Germany alone, sixty-thousand Germans a year immigrated to America during the five years beginning in 1840. That number increased in 1846 to eighty thousand immigrants.[1] So many people tried to leave Europe that there were sometimes not enough ships to carry them. One historian wrote, "Because of the potato famines and other economic hardships, German immigration was so large that immigrants without tickets were warned not to come to Bremen."[2] Bremen was the popular port of embarkation for those leaving Germany.

Henry likely travelled light, taking only the amount of baggage allowed to make the trip. Passengers received detailed lists of the luggage they would need. The shipping company furnished food, mattresses, and cooking utensils, but travelers were advised to pack blankets and other amenities. Emigrants had to bring their own clothing. Women were expected to carry six shifts, two flannel petticoats, six pairs of stockings, two pairs of shoes, and two strong gowns. Men were instructed to have extra trousers, six shirts, six pairs of stockings, two pairs of shoes, and two complete suits. Those who could afford it added extra clothing and food items to make the six-week journey more tolerable.

However, many poor immigrants arrived in America with nothing but a small bag, simply unable to afford more.

Henry Schaumann would have started his journey from his home in Clauen by cart and by foot, either traveling east a few miles to Peine and catching a train to Hanover; or going about the same distance to Hildesheim and going from there by rail. Peine connected to the railroad in 1843, and either route would have passed through the city of Hanover and ultimately to Bremen. At Bremen, he registered and cleared emigration authority.

Certain rules governed. Bremen was the first port city to pass laws designed to improve quality of life for emigrants. Each ship had to be sea worthy, have a minimum amount of space per passenger, and have provisions on board for ninety days at sea. Living spaces were regularly inspected and kept clean. The rules required that a doctor be on board each voyage. A list of passengers had to be furnished by ship owners.

After registering at Bremen, it took a day to go from Bremen to Bremerhaven. Emigrants traveled from Bremen down the Weser River by barge to Brake, and from there by brig on to Bremerhaven, and then out onto the North Sea.

Henry likely sailed in steerage class from Bremerhaven although that is not known. There were three classes of passengers on a typical Bremerhaven ship. Cabin passengers paid the most and enjoyed the most luggage space; intermediate class was a step down from cabin; and steerage class was the least costly and the least amenable. Most emigrants traveled steerage, which provided very little space or privacy on board.

The high demand for travel caused ships ordinarily built for freight purposes to be refitted as passenger ships. A "tween" deck was built and freight space was divided up to accommodate emigrants. Ships were divided into three layered sections. The bottom, or the "hold", carried provisions and baggage; the middle division was steerage; and the upper section contained the cabins. Steerage was partitioned into cubicles that contained upper and lower berths for sleeping, usually five persons to a cubicle. Steerage passengers cooked and ate in communal fashion at a long table with benches on either side. Meals comprised salted pork and beef, peas, beans, barley, rice, potatoes, sauerkraut, and cabbage. Shipping companies enjoyed a lucrative business in emigrant transportation. Passengers paid for travel to America; freight was then loaded for the return trip thus collecting revenue both ways and avoiding the need to load ballast on the outward voyage. Shrewd businessmen hoped to avoid bad weather that could easily double the length of the journey.

Immigrants came to America in large numbers, mostly to escape war and famine but also to start a new life. Among them were artisans and farmers with enough funds to buy land and start businesses. Among the immigrants, also, were political refugees seeking to escape the turmoil in Germany. Henry perhaps came for many reasons. The famine was widespread and persistent, and he was of an age to serve in the military forces of the revolution.

Henry's voyage from Hanover to the United States must be viewed as hypothetical because no proven records have been produced that identify him and confirm exactly when and how he traveled. Nevertheless, the above-described route from Clauen through Bremen and Bremerhaven to America is the most likely route he took because Bremen was the preferred departure point for most German nationals emigrating from Henry's area of Hanover. He could have chosen to leave from Hamburg, another popular immigrant-processing center, but Bremen seems the more likely place. Either way, the registration process and ship passage was the same once aboard ship and in route to America.

Into this air of uncertainty entered one, Heinrich Schumann, a character astonishingly similar to Henry Schaumann both in name and in description. Heinrich Schumann, also of Hanover, sailed from Bremen as one of 255 passengers aboard the Bremen Ship Ernestine, which arrived at the port of New Orleans on June 4, 1850. [3] New Orleans was the point of debarkation for immigrants headed for St. Louis. From New Orleans, it was an easy riverboat ride up the Mississippi River to St. Louis. Schumann listed his age as 24, approximately the same age as Henry Schaumann whose age is calculated to be about 24 in the year 1850. Schumann listed his occupation on the ship passenger list as "tailor." He traveled in steerage class. [4]

A Henry Shoemann appeared in the 1860 US Census living in the Third Ward of St. Louis working as a tailor. At age 37, according to the census, he was unmarried. It is known that Henry Schaumann married in 1863, and would have been likewise unmarried in 1860. Now, if Henry Shoemann the St. Louis tailor is the same as Henry Schumann the tailor who arrived on board the Ernestine, he would have been about 34 and not 37 as the census stated, well-suited by age to be Henry Schaumann who married late at the age of 38 in 1863. He would have been about 34 in 1860.

None of this proves that Schaumann, Schumann, and Shoemann are all one and the same. Nevertheless, only one of them, Henry Shoemann, appeared in the 1860 census living in St. Louis. Either Henry Schaumann was not counted in the census, arrived in St. Louis after 1860, or he was Henry Schoemann, a.k.a. Henry Schumann. The vagaries of census taking in the 19th Century makes this a possibility, particularly in light of the many variations encountered in the spelling of the Schaumann name.[5] Meanwhile, on the minus side, Henry was known to be a laborer and mechanic; nowhere did he mention being a tailor.

Adding to the confusion, St. Louis in the same period as Henry Schaumann was also home to at least four other residents of the name Schaumann or one of its close derivatives: Henry Schaumann of identical spelling, Henry Schuemann, John Henry Schumann, and Henry Schuman. All of these men survived Henry and therefore could not be the same person.[6]

Through the various congruencies of events and remembering the uncertainties young German men faced in war-torn Hanover, it seems reasonable to conclude that Henry arrived in America around 1850. Due to the inconclusiveness of the record, however, it is only possible to say that Henry Schaumann undisputedly first came to light in St. Louis in 1861 when he enlisted as a private in the Union army in the American Civil War.

Old Port of Bremerhaven. This scene at Bremerhaven shows ships lying at anchor awaiting passengers for the journey to America. Emigrants leaving Hanover walked this path to the port administration building at the top of the hill for final processing for the trip across the Atlantic. Passsengers took up residence in crowded tenements that lined the port while awaiting departure. Lithograph *Bremerhaven* by G. Weinhold with the depiction of the office building around 1845. Courtesy of Historical Museum Bremerhaven.

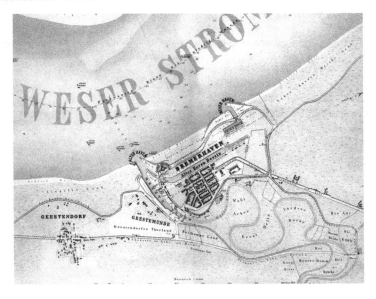

Map of Bremerhaven in 1849. Bremerhaven lies on the east side of the Weser River at the junction of the Weser and the Geest Rivers. Built on land ceded by Hanover, the Old Port (Alter Hafen) was the principal debarkation point from Germany until 1852 when the New Harbor (Neuer Hafen) opened adjacent to it. The Old Harbor was the service point for ships leaving Germany during the time of Henry Schaumann's emigration. G. Hunckel, Der alter hafen in Bremerhaven.

Emigrants at Dinner. An 1847 wood engraving shows steerage passengers seated at long tables eating dinner; bunks line either side. These German immigrants were bound for New Zealand and not America. Accommodations were similar on most immigrant ships and typical of the conditions passengers experienced on a journey to the ports of New York and New Orleans in the mid-19th Century. From the Illustrated London News, 13 April 1844, p. 229.

Page from the Manifest of the Bremen Ship Ernestine. Heinrich Schumann, passenger number 252, arrived at the Port of New Orleans on January 4, 1850. The master of the Ernestine noted that no passengers died on the voyage. National Archives and Records Administration, Washington, D.C.

The Bremen Ship Ernestine. It was the Ernestine that landed at the Port of New Orleans on June 4, 1850. Among its 255 passengers was Heinrich Schumann, a 24-year-old immigrant from Hanover. J. Robinson & G.F. Dow, *The Sailing Ships of New England.* Marine Research Society, 1924.

5

The Civil War and the Germans

The sentiment in St. Louis generally favored neutrality on the secession question; that is, whether the South should leave the United States.[1] Yet the anxiety about it risked the division of the city just as it did the state and nation. The demographics of the city's population threatened to tip the equilibrium to one side or the other. St. Louis took pride in normal times in its traditional southern lifestyle woven into a patchwork of wholesome ethnic diversity. No city could have been more American than St. Louis in 1861.[2] More than 50 percent of the population was immigrant. The citizenry comprised about one-third Irish, one-third native-born American, and one-third German. The Irish immigrant population sided mostly with the native-born residents on sectional issues and with a few notable exceptions favored the South, as did many of the native-born citizens steeped as they were in southern heritage. This group—the Irish and native-born—was about nine to one for the Confederacy and decidedly southern in their sympathy.[3] The Germans, on the other hand, were unquestionably pro-Union and staunchly sided with the North.[4] The only meaningful support Abraham Lincoln received in the 1860 election in Missouri came from the German vote, mostly from St. Louis.

Germans comprised by far the largest ethnic block of the city's immigrant population. Of the eighty-eight thousand Germans living in the state of Missouri in 1860, fifty thousand of them lived in and around St. Louis, accounting for fully one-third of the city's total population.[5]

Many of the Germans were exiled leaders of the failed German Revolution of 1848-1849.[6] Just as the potato famines in Ireland in the 1840s brought 1.5 million new Irish immigrants to America, so did the ravages of war in Germany a decade later

27

bring a new wave of European immigration breaking over the nation's shores. They came as counts, barons, scholars, preachers, and gentleman farmers, carrying with them the last flicker of idealism of the old country.[7]

Although not enthusiastic about fighting for freedom and democracy a second time, the Germans saw secession as a danger to their homes and their lives that left them without a choice. The strident position of the South to preserve slavery made it clear that the only hope for the worker was in the defense of the Union.[8] To improve the prospects of white laborers, the North had to subdue the South, they believed, and Lincoln had to preserve the Union. Otherwise, the South stood to negate the German dream of freedom and jobs for the working person.[9] Moreover, as veterans of the German Revolution, they had fought a losing war to create a centralized federal government that would have abolished feudal domination and the patchwork of monarch-ruled states that comprised 19th Century Germany. Secession now threatened the same outcome in their adopted country. From lessons learned, they wanted no part of a country turned into a patchwork of independent, niggling state sovereignties.[10] They found themselves in a reversal of roles. Usually rebellion wants freedom from an oppressive government. In this case, freedom was the boon of the national authority, and slavery in the sovereign states of the South was the keystone of the uprising.[11] German-Americans saw a parallel between the feudal serfdom they had fled in Germany and slavery in the United States. The southern slave barons reminded them of the feudal lords who denied peasants the right to own land in the fatherland. It was a belief that recalled the historic German resistance to slavery that traced back to the Germantown Quaker opposition of 1688 and the creed that said, "That none of the branch societies [of Germans] shall sanction the legal existence of any kind of aristocracy, and that each shall ever renounce the introduction of slavery."[12]

Germans in St. Louis voiced their opposition to slavery even before the specter of Civil War began.[13] Enmity between Germans and slaveholders was a bitter pill. The last public slave auction held in St. Louis took place when a crowd of Germans shouted down the auctioneer. Slave owners thereafter blamed the Germans with stopping slave auctions. Germans became the target of abuse and terrorism from slave masters and other ethnocentric native Missourians because of the German steadfast rejection of slavery. A large segment of the people spurned anyone of German heritage and ridiculed their cultural habits as well as their politics. Germans considered most St. Louis citizens to be German haters; haters of a class of people on the fringe of St. Louis society that needed to be taught a lesson.[14] The abolitionist politicians of the North, on the other hand, looked upon the German character as the spirit of tolerance and freedom, willing to fight oppression everywhere.

The Germans brought to the Union army a zealousness for war but likewise brought unique qualities of patience, steadiness, and persistence, not only on the battlefield but also in camp, on the march, and in many other tedious situations incidental to military life.[15] They proved to be particularly valuable in the training of the artillery service. The Germans had no special proof of heroism in the excitement of battle or the dangers of combat; many nationalities shared that character of courage. The Germans, however, did give by their example and experience a stability of purpose in the early stages of the war to the masses of impulsive and undisciplined volunteers; the Germans guided youthful warriors in a much-needed spirit of duty and cooperation.

Some said, of course, not too much should be made of German Union patriotism because not all war service is altruistic. Most Germans knew nothing of the circumstances of the US Constitution nor the promises of allegiance to it.[16] As the war went on, large recruitment bounties attracted many young adventurers. Immigrant Europeans especially collected the bounties, sometimes more than once. A German soldier enlisted, deserted, and then enlisted again for another bounty as many times as he could get away with it. Many Germans no doubt were freebooters drawn by the high pay, rapid promotion, and the advantages that come with a volunteer army. Then again, such conduct did not rest solely with one ethnic population.[17]

Did the Germans keep Missouri for the Union? The ramifications of that question are enormous for its impact on the outcome of the Civil War. President Lincoln's call for troops from Missouri would surely have gone unanswered without the Germans. The state's position of armed neutrality might well have extended to the confiscation of federal property and the decommissioning of all US army installations within the borders of the state. Missouri Governor Claiborne Jackson hypothetically would have taken the state out of the Union and joined the

Confederacy. The state consequently would have denied the Union use of the state's industry and resources for the purposes of war. Lincoln's plan to sever the Confederacy along the Mississippi River would have failed and perhaps with it Union victory. The war might have turned out very differently without German American intervention. St. Louis supplied more troops to the Union than any city west of the Mississippi by the war's end, most of them of German heritage.[18] Statewide, thirty-one thousand men from Missouri born in Germany fought on the Union side, representing nearly every Missouri German of military age, almost all of them from St. Louis. The only state fielding more volunteers who were German was New York.

The US Missouri Volunteer regiments comprised three-month service enlistees recruited purposely for the defense of the St. Louis Arsenal to keep it out of the hands of St. Louis rebels. Made up almost entirely of German immigrants, many volunteers still carried German citizenship. [19] They were, in some respects, mercenaries, but Washington saw them as necessary mercenaries under the circumstances. Contrary to what most of the Germans thought; that is, to restrict their military service to the defense of St. Louis and the arsenal. Authorities in Washington envisioned the German service to extend beyond the environs of St. Louis. William Henry Seward, Lincoln's Secretary of State, publicly pronounced, "Missouri is Germanizing itself to make itself free."[20] If Missouri is to remain in the Union, he told a St. Louis audience, the Germans would do it.

St. Louis in 1859. Bird's-eye view of Saint Louis, Missouri, as seen from above the Mississippi River. Lithograph by A. Janicke & Co., St. Louis, Anzeiger des Westens, c. 1859. Library of Congress.

Bird's-eye view of downtown St. Louis from the courthouse dome. The view is looking southwest towards the northwest corner of Fourth and Olive Streets. Photograph by E. Boehl, 1869. Missouri Historical Society.

6

Pvt. Henry Schaumann

On August 10, 1861, the Union Army suffered a major defeat in the young Civil War when 5,340 Union soldiers, mostly Germans, under General Nathaniel Lyon faced off against 12,120 joint Confederate troops and the Missouri state Guard at the Battle of Wilson's Creek, about 12 miles southwest of Springfield, Missouri. [1] General Lyon was killed in the engagement. Union forces withdrew to Springfield and then on to Rolla, Missouri, where they expected to regroup in preparation for further hostilities.

Henry Schaumann enlisted as a Union volunteer on October 14, 1861, three months after Wilson's Creek, probably at the St. Louis Arsenal where General Lyon had initially formed his army of US Reserves before beginning his expedition into southwest Missouri.[2]

Henry was among the earliest enlistees in Captain Michael Laux's Company A of the 1st Regiment, Missouri Artillery, US Reserve Corps Volunteers at St. Louis, under Col. H. Almstedt. Captain Laux began recruiting his company in the fall of 1861 shortly after the Battle of Wilson's Creek. The 1st Regiment was quickly renamed the 2nd Regiment Light Artillery, Union Missouri Volunteers. Not officially organized until January 1862, confusion in the organizational record of Company A later caused problems when Henry could not be found on the rolls of Company A, notwithstanding his service record that showed him present throughout his enlistment period in Battery A of the 2nd Light Artillery.[3]

Assigned first to duty at forts around St. Louis, Company A of the 2nd Light Artillery was attached first to the District of St. Louis, Department of Missouri, and then later to the District of Rolla.[4]

Henry arrived at Rolla in October. His unit went into camp midway between the town of Rolla and Fort Wyman, a fort under construction as part of the vanguard of Union presence against the Confederate-held ground in southwest Missouri.

The Pacific Railroad (later Frisco) tracks had reached Rolla in the early spring of 1861. Col. Franz Sigel's troops secured Rolla on June 14, 1861, as part of a plan to control the rail and river network of Missouri, making the town of Rolla a strategic railhead in the Ozarks situated between St. Louis and Springfield. Following the Union defeat of Gen. Lyon at the Battle of Wilson's Creek, the Union Army retreated to Rolla and began construction of an earthen fort on the top of a hill about two-thirds of a mile south-southwest of the Phelps County Courthouse, at Rolla. The railhead was seen as critical to the Union. President Abraham Lincoln issued an order: "By all means hold Rolla."

Construction of the fort—named Fort Wyman after the local Union commander—began in the latter part of August 1861. Col. Wyman sent out soldiers in all directions from Rolla to round up what he called rebellious residents. They were made prisoners and forced to clear the Fort Wyman area of brush and trees.

The redoubt presented stark contrast to the idyllic countryside in which it was built. It was a rectangle about 300 feet square surrounded by a ditch six feet deep sloping up to an earthen wall 10 feet high built of earth excavated from the enclosing moat. Access to the fort was controlled through a single gate in the north wall. A retractable plank drawbridge crossed the ditch. Artillery positions occupied each corner. Gunners fired off the fort's 32-pound cannons to practice and to mark an occasional celebration. By contrast, to the north of the fort a mile across the valley stood the little village of Rolla. Stretching away in the distance to the east and south were the Ozarks hills. To the west, the eye could make out the meandering path of the Gasconade River.[5]

Rolla, Missouri, was an important site during the Civil War because the southwest branch of the Pacific Railroad ended there. The railroad arrived in Rolla in 1860, but the outbreak of the war halted the westward expansion of the line. According to an article appearing in the *Rolla Daily News*, thousands of Union troops and their supplies came to Rolla by train from St. Louis over the course of the war and then were transferred to wagon trains to go to the battles of Wilson Creek, Pea Ridge, and Prairie

Grove, in Arkansas, plus a number of other smaller skirmishes. After General Lyon was killed at Wilson's Creek, his body was brought to Rolla to be transported by rail back East for burial in Connecticut.

Rolla, a town of about 600 civilians, had a large population of Union troops. Union forces seized control of the town early in the war and had a big impact on the town and its operation. The town was a busy place; business was good. In 1860, sugar sold for 10 cents a pound, tobacco for 30 cents a pound. Whiskey went for 25 cents a gallon. City lots sold for $25 per lot. The courthouse, under construction in 1860, was used as a hay storage barn and later as a hospital for wounded soldiers. Old town Rolla was located along Main Street near the courthouse.

Following the Union defeat at Wilson's Creek, the Union Army fell back to Rolla and began building Fort Wyman. Fort Dette, a second more detailed fort, was constructed later in 1863 a half mile north of the courthouse on what is now the campus of the Missouri University of Science and Technology. Both forts remained in Union hands throughout the Civil War and were never seriously threatened by Confederate forces.

When Henry Schaumann arrived at Rolla, he was assigned to an outpost situated between Rolla and Fort Wyman called Camp Hamilton. There were a number of these camps spread around the countryside, including Camp Halleck named for General Henry Halleck, the Department of the Missouri commandant. Henry's camp was named for General Schuyler Hamilton, grandson of Alexander Hamilton. Both generals went on to distinguish themselves as Union generals. General Halleck was general-in-chief of all U.S. armies before being replaced by General Ulysses Grant.

THE ARSENAL AT ST. LOUIS, MISSOURI.—[SKETCHED BY ALEXANDER SIMPLOT.]

The Federal Arsenal at St. Louis, Missouri. The Arsenal as it appeared at the time of Henry Schaumann's enlistment. Immigrant Germans came here by the thousands to join Union forces at the beginning of the Civil War. Wood engraving by A. Simplot, 1861. *Harper's Weekly*, Aug. 31, 1861.

Flag of Company A, 2nd Regiment Artillery Missouri Volunteers. Painted silk red, white, and blue, with gold stars. Restored 25½" x 42", 1861-1865. This flag is the remnants of the guidon from Henry Schaumann's Company A, 2nd Regiment Artillery. Only about 35 percent of the original flag remains. Missouri State Museum.

Map of Civil War Operations in Missouri, 1861. The Pacific (Frisco) Railroad from St. Louis terminated at Rolla, Missouri. Map from Jacob Wells, "Operations in Missouri, 1861," in *Battles and Leaders of the Civil War*, Vol. 1, 1887.

Sketch of Fort Wyman, Rolla, Missouri. This drawing shows Fort Wyman approximately as it appeared when Henry Schaumann was posted there in the fall of 1862. No photograph of the fort is known to exist. *Frank Leslie's Illustrated Newspaper*, Feb. 1, 1862. Missouri Historical Markers.

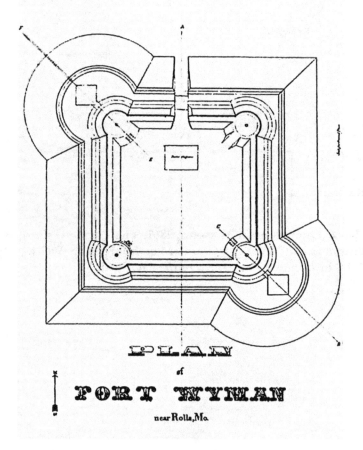

Plan of Fort Wyman, near Rolla, Missouri. Four 32-pounder cannons hauled from the railhead at Rolla by a ten-mule team stood at each corner of the fort. National Archives and Records Administration, Washington, D.C. Missouri Historical Markers.

Camp of 36" Illinois Regt. Rolla Mo.

A Soldier's Sketch of a Camp at Fort Wyman, Rolla, Missouri, c. 1862. This camp of the 36th Illinois Regiment was at Fort Wyman at about the same time Henry Schaumann was encamped at Camp Hamilton. The artist drew the US Flag upside down. Lyman Gibson Bennett Diary - Dec 21, 1861 to April 4, 1862, p. 26. Missouri Secretary of State Archives.

7

Accident at Fort Wyman

P vt. Henry Schaumann's duties were those of an artillery
private. There were the usual troop duties a soldier was
expected to discharge as part of a garrison unit. Such an
assignment occurred at Camp Hamilton while Henry's unit was
bivouacked along the Pacific Railroad midway between Rolla and
Fort Wyman. Around October 1, Henry was sent to fetch water
for washing and drinking purposes. The terrain around Rolla is
hilly and, at that time, was etched by numerous spring-fed
streams that coursed through the countryside. While carrying
water, Henry accidentally fell striking a stump and seriously
injuring his right abdomen. Different accounts say he fell into a
hollow near the railroad, others say that he was jumping a ditch
or creek and fell back onto a stump. Over the years, family
tradition remembered that he was thrown from his horse when
the horse stumbled jumping a stream. In any event, he fell with
such an injurious impact that it left him incapacitated.[1] He
checked into the post hospital where he remained hospitalized
for a month unable to rejoin his unit.

Examination by the regiment surgeon found him incapable of
performing the duties of a soldier because of a femoral hernia of
the right side received accidentally by falling into the ditch. The
surgeon determined that the injury disabled henry one-half from
obtaining his subsistence by manual labor, in the surgeon's
opinion.[2] Based on the examining surgeon's report, Henry was
determined to be physically unfit for service, and was given an
honorable disability discharge.

Henry's honorable discharge from duty was approved by order
of Brigadier General Samuel R. Curtis, Department of the
Missouri Headquarters, St. Louis, on November 22, 1862, and
carried out two days later on the 24th by Lt. Col Harry Graham,

post commander at Rolla. Henry gathered his belongings, boarded the train, and returned to St. Louis.

Because of his disability, Henry was eligible for an invalid pension. On December 16, 1862, he was re-examined at St. Louis. The surgeon reaffirmed after careful examination that because of a femoral hernia, Henry was one-half incapacitated from obtaining his subsistence by manual labor. Furthermore, the surgeon determined that "judging from his present condition, and from the evidence before me, it is my belief that the said disability arose...in the line of duty. The disability is of a permanent character...His disability is likely to be permanent unless surgical means of relief are resorted to."[3] On December 26, 1862, Henry's discharge was officially recorded in the Adjutant General's Office, thus ending his brief military career and beginning the legal process to obtain a military invalid pension.

Meanwhile, Henry had evaded matrimony for nearly 40 years. In the winter of 1863, he developed a romantic relationship with a young German immigrant named Margarethe Ficke. Like him, she was from The Kingdom of Hanover. She was 26 years old; he was age 38. It was her second marriage.[4]

The couple set up housekeeping on Third Street between Convent and Rugers Streets, taking their place as the latest immigrant family to call St. Louis home.[5]

Despite being older than Margarethe, Henry was still a relatively young man but because of his disability was unable to work full time. A lot of the future rode on him getting a military pension.

Military pensions were not automatic. With his disability discharge and the surgeon's report in hand Henry secured the services of Randolph Mackwitz, a St. Louis attorney, to prosecute his claim and do the things necessary to obtain an invalid pension.

The application required, in addition to a detailed declaration of Henry's disability, sworn statements from those who knew him and could attest to the veracity of his claim, and that he was indeed the identical Henry Schaumann who enlisted in the United States service on October 14, 1861. One of the "wholly disinterested" witnesses to his application as required by law was Henry Rauch whose wife Sophia was the sister of Henry Schaumann's newly acquired bride Margarethe.

The application for pension was drawn up on February 2,

1863, in the office of the clerk of the St. Louis Circuit Court. Attorney Mackwitz pointed out in his narrative that Henry was "a mechanic by occupation, but by reason of his injury one-half disabled from obtaining his subsistence by manual labor" and that he had had "no occupation since leaving the service." He added that the claimant's habits were "temperate," a quality appreciated if not required by the Pension Office.[6]

Henry's application was sent to the Pension Office, and on August 29, 1863, his claim was admitted and approved at one-half disability by femoral hernia of the right side in the pension amount of $4.00 per month, commencing retroactive to November 24, 1862, the date of Henry's discharge from the service.[7] A single hernia was by law allowed a $4.00 pension, one-half of the maximum $8.00 set by statute for a double hernia. Retroactive to November under the law Henry was due a lump sum of $36.00, a good amount for a newlywed, and soon-to-be father.

Rolla, Missouri, in the 1860s. The Phelps
County Courthouse stands on the left. Henry
Schaumann was here in 1862 stationed at
nearby Fort Wyman. *Ozarks Watch.* Vol. 6, No.
3, Winter 1993.

Phelps County Courthouse under Construction, Rolla,
Missouri, 1860. Completed in 1862-63, the courthouse was
used as a hospital by Union forces. *Ozarks Watch.* Vol. 6,
No. 3, Winter 1993.

8	2 L. Art'y.	Mo.

Henry Schaumann

Priv., 1st Battery A, 2 Reg't Mo. L. Art'y.

Appears on

Battery Muster Roll

for *Sept & Oct*, 186 *2*

Present or absent *Absent*

Stoppage, $ 100 for

Due Gov't, $ 100 for

Valuation of horse, $ 100

Valuation of horse equipments, $ 100

Remarks: *Absent sick in Post Hospl Rolla Mo. since the 24ʳ of Oct 1862*

Book mark:

(358)   Copyist.

H. S. Brandon

8	2 L. Art'y.	Mo.

H. Schaumann

Priv., 1st Battery A, 2 Reg't Mo. L. Art'y.

Appears on

Battery Muster Roll

for *From Aug 31 to Dec 31*, 186 *2*

Present or absent

Stoppage, $ 100 for

Due Gov't, $ 100 for

Valuation of horse, $ 100

Valuation of horse equipments, $ 100

Remarks: *Dischgd for disability on the 24ʳ of Nov. 1862*

See Batty M.O.R.

Book mark:

(358)   Copyist.

H. S. Brandon

Battery Muster Roll Records for Henry Schaumann. "Absent sick in Post Hosptl. Rolla, Mo. Since the 24th of Oct. 1862."; "Dischgd for disability on the 24th of Nov. 1862." Service Record, National Archives, Washington, D.C.

Disability Discharge of Pvt. Henry Schaumann, dated November 24, 1862. Service Record, National Archives, Washington, D.C.

8

The St. Louis Cholera Epidemic of 1866

Henry and Margarethe Schaumann made their home at 1259 South Third Street. They managed a living on Henry's pension, work Margarethe took in as a seamstress, and what jobs Henry was able to do.[1] The hostilities of the Civil War were in full swing but had so far bypassed St. Louis, although the conflict had seriously affected the city's economy as it had every other part of the country. Nevertheless, it seemed a safe enough time to start a family. On November 21, 1863, baby Friedrich Henry Schaumann was born.

On April 9, 1865, Robert E. Lee surrendered his Army of Northern Virginia, ending the long bitter struggle of the South to secede from the Union. The St. Louis economy began a gradual return to normalcy as steamships once again plied the Mississippi River, safe to deliver their goods to the St. Louis port. A heavy influx of people strained the public resources, infrastructure lagged behind, and pollution accumulated in certain parts of the city.

Cholera made its appearance in St. Louis during the last week of July 1866, being brought there by rail from New York City.[2] Nearly a year before, Missouri Governor T.C. Fletcher had called the attention of the St. Louis authorities to the necessity of preparing for a cholera outbreak, but nothing was done. The cholera was not in St. Louis, they replied, and it was argued that any measures of preparation for it would frighten away strangers and injure business. The city's Board of Health in 1866 consisted of a health officer and a committee from the City Council, but it had very little authority. The outbreak of cholera in July of 1866 found the board wholly unprepared to deal with the pestilence.

Cholera is an acute bacterial infection of the intestine. Symptoms include acute watery diarrhea and vomiting which can result in severe dehydration. When left untreated, death can occur rapidly. A person may get cholera by drinking water or eating food contaminated with the cholera bacterium. The disease can spread rapidly in areas with inadequate treatment of sewage and drinking water.[3] The cholera bacterium may also live in the environment in brackish rivers and coastal waters. The disease is not likely to spread directly from one person to another; therefore, casual contact with an infected person is not a risk for becoming ill. It is wholly dependent on unhealthy living conditions.

When the cholera did strike, its effect soon escalated to epidemic proportions. Five deaths occurred in St. Louis during the first week of its existence, and then it broke out in a dozen places at once. For three weeks, or until vigorous and systematic measures were taken to fight it, the epidemic grew at an alarming rate. There were 120 fatal cases the second week, 754 the third, and 991 the fourth—the week in which Henry Schaumann died. The epidemic did not amount to much after September, only 51 deaths occurred in the city in October and only 4 in November. August was the worst month; 2,388 fatal cases of cholera occurred in that month. In September, the number was 1,082. By this time a committee of citizens had been organized in each ward, the houses of the infected districts visited, and the patients furnished with rooms and medicine. The mortality then began to fall and it continued to steadily decline until it ceased altogether. The total fatalities for the 1866 St. Louis epidemic numbered 3,527.

The epidemic was worse in those portions of the city that had the least access to sanitary measures. "Bohemia" and Frenchtown—or Germantown as the latter was sometimes called—fared about as badly as any portion of the city. More than 43 percent of the fatalities occurred in the river districts east of Broadway Avenue between the Arsenal and Biddle Street. The highest concentration (951 deaths) was in an area between Market Street and Biddle, east of Broadway in the river front district centered on Laclede's Landing in the vicinity of the present day Jefferson Expansion Memorial (Gateway Arch). Of the 1,538 deaths recorded in this region of the city, 312 fatal cases occurred in the district east of Broadway and between Chouteau Avenue and the Arsenal,[4] the area in which the Schaumann family lived. The Schaumann family lived on Third Street between Convent and Rutgers in one of the hardest hit regions, situated north of the arsenal and less than a mile south of Market Street. The Schaumanns were in the direct path of the epidemic.

The epidemic spread west from Broadway. Fatalities occurred in 615 different blocks and districts covering about one-fourth of the entire city of St. Louis, which at that time had a population of 204,000 inhabitants. The prevailing death rate in the more thickly populated portions of the city was between 10 and 20 percent, although in a few sections it got up to 25 percent with cholera killing one in every four people. That same year (1866) 5,379 residents died in St. Louis of causes other than cholera, altogether claiming about 5 percent of the population of the city in a single year.

Conflicting causes of death were given for Henry Schaumann including consumption (an old term for tuberculosis) and cholera.[5] The St. Louis City Death Register gave his cause of death as Cholera.[6] The date of his death was August 20, 1866, during the height of the cholera epidemic. Tuberculosis and the femoral hernia that had led in 1862 to his disability discharge from the Civil War likely complicated the cause of his death.

A femoral hernia is a loop of intestine, or another part of the abdominal contents, that has been forced out of the abdomen through a channel called the femoral canal, a tube-shaped passage at the top of the front of the thigh. The loop is usually only the size of a grape. A femoral hernia can cause serious medical problems if left untreated, even if there are no troublesome symptoms to begin with. Treatment is by an operation to return the herniated intestine to its proper place and close the weakness in the abdominal wall. There is no indication that Henry ever underwent corrective surgery.

The femoral canal, through which a femoral hernia is squeezed, is next to the point where the blood vessels and nerves pass from the abdomen into the leg. It is a potential weak spot in the abdominal wall. The intestine or the tissue that covers it is more likely to be forced out through the femoral canal if a weakness already exists. An increase in the pressure inside the abdomen by activities such as standing up, coughing or straining can then trigger a hernia. A sharp blow to the stomach, such as striking a stump in Henry's case, also can cause one. Other factors that make a femoral hernia more likely to develop include carrying or pushing heavy loads, such as carrying heavy buckets of water, which was Henry's duty assignment when he was injured.

If the hernia can be manually pushed back into the abdomen, it is referred to as "reducible". However, usually this is not possible and the hernia is effectively stuck in the canal. This is an "irreducible" hernia and is a potentially dangerous condition. The blood supply to the herniated tissue can become crushed within the canal, cutting off its source of oxygen and nutrients. This is known as a strangulated hernia and emergency surgery must be performed to release the trapped tissue and restore its blood supply. A strangulated hernia is very painful and tender to the touch. All femoral hernias need to be treated surgically to avoid the high risk of becoming strangulated. A strangulated intestine can result in gangrene, a life-threatening condition requiring emergency surgery. Cases were relatively common during the Civil War and a complication from femoral hernia was listed on more than one occasion as cause of death. Pension applications are known to have involved claims directly related to femoral hernia. Articles regarding treatment of femoral hernia appeared during and shortly after the War.[7]

According to Margarethe Schaumann, Henry's wife, Henry died on a Monday at home at 1259 South Third Street, not far from the St. Louis waterfront.[8] However, his name was entered in the City Death Register as "Hy Schumann," born in Germany and residing in St. Louis on Gratitot Street. The register entry is an enigma that questions whether Henry died at home. It opens the possibility that he may not have been at home at the time. Despite her claim in Henry's pension papers that he died at home, a different statement by Margarethe preserved in family oral history adds credibility that he died elsewhere. "I did not know he was as ill as he was," she is alleged to have said, "or I would have gone to him."[9]

Gratitot Street intersected with Third Street about four blocks northeast of the Schaumann address. Gratiot ran west from the waterfront, and it is possible that Henry had moved from the Third Street address given in his Civil War papers. The Gratiot and Third Street intersection of his time is today's Interstate 55 just south of Exit 209B. This was also the approximate location of the McDowell medical building.

Henry was about 40 years old when he died. He was buried the following Thursday, August 23, 1866, at Holy Ghost Cemetery, in St. Louis. In his pension documents, his widow, Margarethe, gave the date of August 23 as his date of death.

Cemetery records show, however, that August 23 was the date of his interment.[10]

On the October 14, 1861, Civil War enlistment form, Henry gave his age as 37. On his signed pension application, dated February 2, 1863, two years later, his age was again listed as 37. Meanwhile, the St. Louis Death Register recorded his age as age 40 on August 20, 1866. Accordingly, he was born between 1824 and 1826, but most likely 1826 congruent with his date of enlistment and date of death. In any event, Henry was at least ten years older than his wife, Margarethe, who was age 30 when Henry died.

Meanwhile, young Friedrich Henry Schaumann was not yet three years old when his father died. It is unknown what circumstances or living conditions, which caused the cholera epidemic of 1866, contributed to the elder Henry's death, and yet spared Margarethe and their son.

Pollution in St. Louis in 1866. Unhealthy conditions within the city fed the cholera epidemic of 1866. *St. Louis Post-Dispatch* Archives.

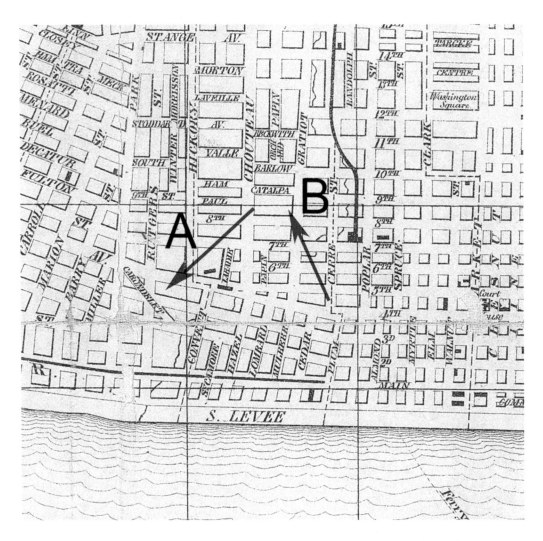

Map of the St. Louis Riverfront. Arrows show the location of the Schaumann residence at 1259 South Third Street (A), and the location of the McDowell Hospital at 8th Street and Gratiot Street (B) where Henry Schaumann died. Also shown is the location of the Iron Mountain Railroad that ran parallel to the levee and the Pacific Railroad that originated a few blocks from the Schaumann residence and proceeded west toward Rolla, Missouri. Map is oriented with north to the right. Modified Kennedy's Sectional Map of St. Louis. R. V. Kennedy & Co., 1859. St. Louis Public Library.

9

Gratiot and Holy Ghost Cemetery

The controversy over exactly where Henry Schaumann died is of little consequence in his story. Nevertheless, the Gratiot location entered on his death certificate and the terse entry that said only "Gratiot" without a specific address suggested that it identified a commonly understood site in St. Louis. The most recognizable location by that name was the old Gratiot Prison, a Union Civil War detention center that also doubled as a hospital.

Many stories are told about Gratiot (pronounced grass-shut). The building that became Gratiot Street Prison originally housed the McDowell Medical College at the corner of Eighth and Gratiot Streets. Adjoining Gratiot Street Prison to the north was the Christian Brothers Academy.

Dr. Joseph McDowell started his medical school in St. Louis in 1840 as the Medical Department of Kemper College. A brilliant physician, he grew the department from its modest beginnings to one of the premier medical schools in the nation. Notwithstanding its reputation for excellence, McDowell's school was a place where wild rumors, lurid stories and eccentricities drew attention to its notorious side. McDowell was described as having a disposition that approached insanity. He hated immigrants and Catholics and would harangue those subjects at street corners wearing a breastplate of armor. He was best known in the city perhaps for the art of body snatching, all night forays into cemeteries to gather specimens for his anatomy classes. Horrified local residents superstitiously avoided the college. Many to this day consider it a haunted place.

McDowell was an ardent supporter of slavery and took the side of the South on the secession question. When Civil War hostilities broke out and it was clear that St. Louis would hold for the

Union, he closed the college and went south to serve the Confederacy. In November 1861, the Union command took over the McDowell building and converted it into a prison for captured Confederate soldiers.

The building, made of rock, consisted of a three-story octagonal tower with two wings, one on either side of the tower. The hospital was on the upper floor of the northern wing. The hospital contained 76 bunks. As sick and wounded prisoners overflowed into the prison, more rooms were converted into additional hospital space.[1]

The prison became a horrible place. The prisoner population soared. Sanitary conditions declined, smallpox broke out, and prisoners died at an alarming rate.

When the war ended, the prison was closed down. McDowell returned to St. Louis to start up his school again. In 1866 when the cholera epidemic struck, medical facilities across the city were taxed to the limit. McDowell, for all his erratic behavior, was known for his generous treatment of the poor and the sick. He was a dedicated physician. When the St. Louis death register of 1866 refers to "Gratiot" as the place of death of Henry Schaumann, it is easily interpreted as a reference to the Gratiot hospital, a holdover name for McDowell Medical College after the Civil War. McDowell did not live to see his school rise to the status that it once claimed in the medical community. He died of pneumonia in 1868. The building fell into disrepair and was later torn down in 1882.

Henry Schaumann was buried at Holy Ghost Cemetery, like many of the victims of the 1866 epidemic, but that would not be his final resting place. He appears on the Holy Ghost Cemetery burial register as "Hy Shannon" buried 23 August 1866, lot #619.[2] The Schaumann name is misspelled—as it was in other official records pertaining to his life and death.[3]

Holy Ghost Cemetery—known also as Old Pickers Cemetery—was opened in 1845 by the German Evangelical Protestant Church of the Holy Ghost as the Holy Ghost Evangelical and Reformed Cemetery, near Arsenal and Gravois Streets. However, it was known most of the time as Old Pickers because that was the name of the church's pastor at the time the cemetery opened.[4] The cemetery was located northwest of the intersection of Wyoming Street and Gravois Road, a 20-acre plot where many victims of the great cholera epidemics of 1849, 1854, and 1866 were interred.[5] The last burial there was in 1901. The present-day Roosevelt High School sets on the original cemetery site.

Over the years, the city had ordered Holy Ghost Cemetery closed several times, but the ordinance was not enforced until July 1916 when the city ordered remains to be removed.[6] After burials ended, all bodies initially buried there were removed to a lot in Zion Cemetery on St. Charles Rock Road. Other bodies had been previously removed to New St. Marcus, Bellefontaine, St. Peter's Evangelical, and New Pickers cemeteries. After 1917 all were removed to Zion.[7]

New Pickers eventually took the name Old Pickers but it is not the same as the original Holy Ghost-Old Pickers. This is confusing. New Pickers was opened in 1862. Sometimes called the Independent Evangelical Protestant Cemetery, it was located at 7133 Gravois Road, six miles from the Court House, near the river Des Peres and was not associated with the Holy Ghost Cemetery.

The removal of burial remains at Holy Ghost Cemetery was not well documented, and records seem not to exist. Genealogists have not been able to determine where many of the remains were re-interred.

The Archaeological Research Center of St. Louis wrote, "I am afraid I will not be of very much help to you concerning Henry Schaumann's burial location. Unfortunately, we have found that in nearly every case where cemeteries have been closed and the bodies supposedly exhumed, the headstones are gone, but the bodies have always been left behind...it is very likely that bodies, including Schaumann, are still at Roosevelt High School. Record keeping and care of burying people does not appear to have been very precise at most graveyards in the 19th Century. Emphasis was placed on above ground appearances. It is generally common that headstones were placed over the wrong graves. So even when families paid for and watched for the removal of a grave, it is likely that the wrong body was removed...I am afraid it is very likely that he is still at the high school."[8]

St. Louis Public Schools ordered the acquisition of property to construct a New Southside High School in 1922. Because there was no vacant land in the area, the Old Pickers Cemetery (Holy Ghost Cemetery) was acquired for the school's site. Evacuation of its graves began in October 1922.[9] "Most graves were relocated to mass graves in other cemeteries, although some remains were not relocated."[10]

According to family tradition, Louise Zinner Eilers, stepdaughter of Henry Schaumann, witnessed the reburial of Henry's remains. No date has been preserved of that event. Stories passed down recount that no remains were recovered; only a few buttons and nonperishable items were found, confirming a common view that the removal and re-interment procedure was tragically careless and insensitive, not to mention undocumented.

Removal of bodies from Holy Ghost cemetery began as early as 1893; it is likely, however, that the re-interment of Henry's remains occurred closer to the 1922 removal date when Louise was in her mid-fifties; if in fact his body was ever properly exhumed from its original burial site at all.

Meanwhile, four thousand five-hundred miles away across the Atlantic Ocean on September 20, 1866—a month to the day after the death of Henry Schaumann—the Kingdom of Hanover ceased to exist; Henry's old birthplace was annexed by Prussia.

McDowell Medical College, St. Louis. The college was confiscated by Union forces and turned into a Confederate prison from 1861 until the end of the war in 1865. It was likely used as a hospital during the 1866 cholera epidemic. Photograph by E. Boehl, 1868.

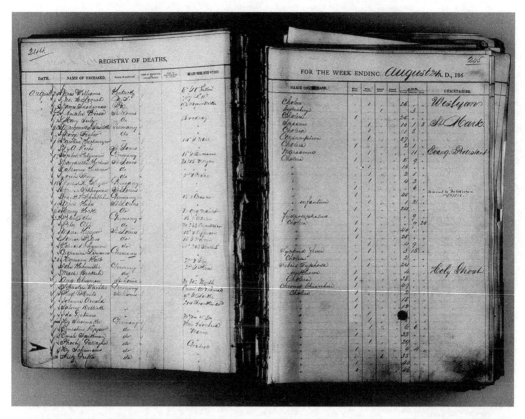

St. Louis Registry of Deaths. The list of deaths for the week of August 24, 1866, included Henry Schaumann, entered as the second name from the bottom as Hy Schumann. His date of death was August 20, 1866. The entry included Germany as his place of nativity; the locality where death occurred was Gratiot; the name of the disease that was the cause of death was cholera; his age at the time of death was 40 years and four months, which calculates his birthday to be April 20, 1826. The cemetery was entered as Holy Ghost. St. Louis (Independent City) Register of deaths, 1850-1909, Vol. 1, January 1866—October 1867, p. 244, Missouri Bureau of Vital Statistics.

Holy Ghost Evangelical Church on Eighth and Walnut Streets. The church opened in 1858. Henry Schaumann was buried in the cemetery associated with this church. Eden Theological Seminary Archives.

Roosevelt High School, St. Louis, in 1937. The school was built on ground   originally occupied by the Holy Ghost Cemetery. Photograph by W.C. Persons. Missouri Historical Society.

10

Margarethe Dorothea Ficke

Margarethe Dorothea Ficke was born May 21, 1836, in St. Hülfe, Diepholz, Hanover, Germany. What may be said about the cultural heritage of Henry Schaumann applies equally to Margarethe; both were born and grew to adulthood in the Kingdom of Hanover at the beginning of the era of Queen Victoria and the end of Hanover's joint rule with Great Britain.

Margarethe was the youngest of three sisters, all born in St. Hülfe.[1] The oldest, Lisette Friederike Ficke, was born November 12, 1830. The middle sister, Wilhelmine Sophia Ficke, was born March 5, 1833.[2]

Sophia was the first to immigrate to America, followed by Margarethe. Sophia and Margarethe remained close throughout their lives. Nothing is known about Lisette who apparently stayed in Germany.

They were the daughters of Johann Friedrich Ficke and Margarethe Luise Brunch Ficke. Johann, born on December 18, 1801, was originally from Aschen, Diepholz, later settling in St. Hülfe, his wife's hometown. Margarethe Luise was born in St. Hülfe about 1802. Johann Ficke's family is traced back five generations to the 17th Century.[3] Each succeeding generation lived in various precincts within the district of Diepholz.

The history of the Ficke family name goes back much further. The name in that region of Europe was common as early as the 15th Century.

In the 1852 Hanover Census there were Fickes also residing in the county of Hoya. Hoya was an ancient state of the old Holy Roman Empire, which today belongs to the district of Diepholz, providing supporting evidence of Diepholz as the ancient seat of the Ficke family.

St. Hülfe, Diepholz, Hanover, refers to the village of St. Hülfe, in the county of Diepholz, in the Kingdom of Hanover. While it is certain that the Ficke family of the mid-19th Century hailed from the Kingdom of Hanover and the county of Diepholz, a more precise location requires interpretation of hand-written records in sometimes careless penmanship. St. Hülfe, for example, is often written in English as St. Huelpe. The umlauted ü of St. Hülfe becomes ue and the f is mistaken for a p, thus St. Hülfe becomes St. Huelpe. Similarly, Margarethe's marriage record has her hailing from "St. Gülfe, in Diepholz." This record is clearly written as St. Gülfe. St. Hülfe appears to have been entered by the scribe as St. Gülfe. However, there was no town in Diepholz, or anywhere else in Hanover, with the name St. Gülfe.

The history of Diepholz is interwoven with that of Diepholz castle and the various rulers who occupied it over the centuries.[4] The castle is relatively small, consisting of three buildings and a modest tower. Today it is the district's courthouse. Construction at the castle site began as early as 980. The castle proper, however, appears to have begun in the first half of the 12th Century. It was completed in 1160. The builder named it "Deefholt," which translated from the Old Saxon means shimmering forest, because it stood in a forest on marshy moorland. The castle stood as the seat of government of the Bishopric of Osnabrück as well as Minden for a brief time. Both Minden and Osnabrück were military Bishoprics that were established by Charlemagne in the 9th Century in an effort to secure control over the Saxon wilderness of northern Germany. By 1097 the family von Diepholz was the official ruling family of the district. A succession of descendants followed as members of the von Diepholz family married members of the local nobility. By the 13th Century, the nobility included the Princess of Sweden, Irmgard von Diepholz, who married the Count of Oldenburg in the late 13th Century. She was great-great-grandmother to Christian I, King of Denmark, thus tracing a direct line of succeeding generations to the Hanoverian George I of England.

Agriculture was the driving force of the Diepholz economy, supplemented increasingly by trade. During the 14th Century, an agricultural market town developed around the castle. The town was granted a city charter in 1380.

The rule of the Diepholz family continued through the 15th Century despite major schisms over Bishoprics of the region and ecclesiastical politics.

The early 16th Century saw the Protestant Reformation take hold, and new protestant churches were built in the region. The castle fell into disrepair during this period but was fully reconstructed around 1550.

As it progressively lost its grip on its ancestral seat of power, the Diepholz family influence shifted to other quarters of the district. Irmgard II von Diepholz was chosen as Princess-Abbess of Essen in 1561, during the reign of Elizabeth I of England. The Abbey of Essen, lying southwest of Diepholz towards the Dutch border, was at that time the largest single landowner in the German Empire, and the Princess-Abbess wielded both ecclesiastical and secular power.

The last Count to reside in the Diepholz castle was Friedrich II who married Anastasia, Countess of Waldeck. They had one daughter, Anna Margarethe. Friedrich died in 1585 at the age of 30. Anna Margarethe married Phillip III, Prince of Hesse, in 1610, effectively sealing the end of the von Diepholz dynasty of rulers as eponymous of the district. Anna Margarethe died in 1629, leaving to succeeding generations the legacy of her name; the name Margarethe grew to be among the most popular names in Diepholz.

Over the next two centuries, Diepholz grew under the rule of the Kingdom of Hanover. When Hanover fell under the Prussian invasion of 1866, Diepholz was absorbed within it. Margarethe Ficke immigrated to America well before 1866 so her German address never included Prussia. She later added Prussia as her country of origin but continued to refer to herself as being originally from Hanover.

At the beginning of the 16th Century, an attempt was made by the powerful duchy of Brunswick-Lüneburg to annex smaller states like Diepholz. However, by forming an alliance with the neighboring state of Hoya and asking help from the emperor of Hanover himself, the state of Diepholz managed to survive until 1585 when the ruling family became extinct with the premature death of Friedrich II. Diepholz eventually came under the administrative rule of Brunswick-Lüneburg. Notwithstanding its political misfortune, the people of Diepholz continued to refer to themselves as being from the state of Diepholz and not Brunswick-Lüneburg, although Diepholz would not officially become the district of Diepholz for another hundred years after Margarethe's time. The modern district of Diepholz was established in 1932 by merging the districts of the former Diepholz and Sulingen. The former Diepholz was roughly identical to the earldom of the medieval state, while the Sulingen district had been a part of the earldom of Hoya. The Diepholz of Margarethe Ficke's time was essentially the geography of the middle ages with a few minor changes in political boundaries.

Known today for its machine industry dedicated to the building of locomotives, the Diepholz area is nevertheless historically agricultural. The residents' main income still comes from farming. The area is essentially rural.

The city of Diepholz is midpoint between Bremen and Osnabrück. Immediately to the south of Diepholz is Lake Dümmer, a lake of around 10 square miles surrounded by ferns and reeds that are the breeding ground of many rare bird species. Creeks and small streams crisscross the district. To the west lie the Dammer Berge Mountains, which are more on the scale of hills than mountains. Forests and farmland cover the northern portions of the district. Like most of northern Germany, the area around the city of Diepholz is generally flat interspersed with areas of marsh.

The town of St. Hülfe borders the city of Diepholz on the north. Today, it is a suburb of Diepholz. Nevertheless, as late as 1866, it stood as an independent village outside its larger metropolitan neighbor. St. Hülfe today is a town of about 1,000 residents and covers an area of approximately six square miles. In Margarethe Ficke's day the village was much smaller, located a comfortable distance out in the countryside. Today it is situated within the metropolitan area of the city of Diepholz.

Traveling from the Ficke home near Diepholz and going north for about 40 miles, one comes to the harbor city of Bremen, located at the mouth of the Weser River. Bremen was one of the main emigration centers of Germany where thousands of young Germans made arrangements for ship passage to America.

The mid-19th Century in Diepholz was a particularly difficult time. Germany was a country trying to recover from the Revolution of 1848-1849. There were few opportunities for German youth. Obtaining food and the necessities of life strained the resources of many families. Stories that reached Hanover about America painted a picture of a land that beckoned immigrants to share the bounty of its promised riches.

Upon arrival at Bremen, emigrants were registered and names entered on a ship's manifest. From Bremen, the next leg of an emigrant's journey was to travel by train or boat 85 miles down the Weser River to the Port of Bremerhaven on the shore of the North Sea. Prior to 1837, ships left directly from the crowded harbor at Bremen before a new embarkation point opened at Bremerhaven.

An emigrant who could afford it checked into one of the emigrant houses at Bremerhaven and waited for a departure date. On the appointed embarkation day, once loaded with its human cargo, the ship sailed out onto the North Sea, and then across the Atlantic Ocean to America. Oftentimes multiple ships departed on the same day.

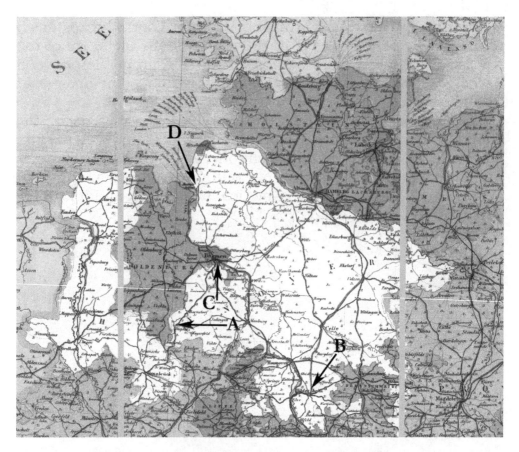

Map of Hanover, Germany. Arrows indicate key locations in the Schaumann-Ficke homeland. (A) Home of Margarethe Ficke at Diepholz; (B) Home of Henry Schaumann at Clauen, near Peine; (C) Emigration harbor at Bremen on the Weser River; and (D) Port of Bremerhaven on the North Sea from which emigrants embarked on their journeys to America. Adapted from a map by J. Perthes, 1855. Library of Congress.

Diepholz Castle. Built from 1120-1160, the castle is a historic landmark of the city of Diepholz. It was a popular attraction in Margarethe Fick's time. Photograph by Günther Leineweber, 1980.

Port of Bremerhaven. An 1848 painting pictures the busy emigrant port of Bremerhaven, Germany, eleven years after the port's founding in 1837. By 1850 more than 2.2 million residents of the United States were immigrants. Many of them embarked from Bremerhaven. *Bremerhaven* by C.J. Fedeler, 1848. Bremen Fockemuseum.

The Emigrant's House at Bremerhaven. German emigrants stayed in waiting halls until the day their ship departed. This hall was built by Heinrich Müller, the shipping magnate, in 1849. Lithograph by W. Casten. Historisches Museum Bremerhaven.

11

Immigrant Sisters

Nothing is known about the Ficke sisters as they were growing up in Hanover.

Sometime before her 23rd birthday, Wilhelmine Sophia Ficke—the middle of the three Ficke sisters—left home for America. We do not know if she traveled alone, but it was common for young women of her age to make the long ship voyage unaccompanied.

The first evidence of Sophia in America comes from the record of her marriage in St. Louis, Missouri. She married Henry Rauch before St. Louis Justice of the Peace Frederick Flack on December 31, 1856.[1] "Red" Rauch, as Henry was nicknamed, was a brick maker-sometimes mason by profession. He was from Hesse-Darmstadt, Germany, when he did not claim an origin in the province of Kur Hessen, formerly Hesse-Kassel prior to its annexation by Prussia in 1866. The two provinces were at one time part of the same geographic region of the Holy Roman Empire in west-central Germany, located outside the southern border of the Kingdom of Hanover.

Sophia and Henry Rauch settled into a home in the Third Ward of St. Louis, on the city's east side in a community of young professionals, many from Germany. Ward Three by coincidence was the same ward where Henry Schaumann lived.

Mr. Rauch was older than Sophia by several years; he was age 32 at the time of their marriage, she was 23.[2]

We may correctly assume that Margarethe and Sophia had not seen each other for at least four years since they were last together at Diepholz.

In the spring of 1859, Margarethe sailed out onto the North Sea to follow her sister to America.

Margarethe's shipboard companion was Friedrich Ewe, a young man from Westfalen. Friedrich Wilhelm Ewe was born August 25, 1833, in Katholisch, Loewen, Province of Westfalen, in the original Free State of Prussia, the son of Ludewig Ewe and Anna Maria Beller Ewe. [3] Just how long Margarethe and Friedrich may have known each other in Germany we do not know. Friedrich was a tailor by profession and may have engaged in that trade in Westfalen. In their early twenties and faced with the growing hardships and uncertainties that confronted many young German families in the 1850s, they decided to leave Germany, possibly at the invitation and with the encouragement of Sophia and Henry Rauch. Sophia had immigrated four years earlier, married, and settled in St. Louis.

So, in the spring of 1859, Friedrich and Margarethe departed for America bound for St. Louis aboard the Bremen ship Olbers. The couple traveled as Friedrich Ewe and Margarethe Ewe, embarking from Bremen and arriving at the Port of New Orleans on June 11, 1859. Their names are found on a debarkation manifest for the Port of New Orleans.[4]

Their journey across the Atlantic on the Olbers was like thousands of similar trips taken by German immigrants in the 19th Century. The ship Olbers was built at Bremerhaven and launched in 1851. It was a two-deck transport, 141 feet in length with a beam of 33 feet six inches, a relatively small vessel compared to the many larger ones that carried emigrants to North America. The Olbers sailed under a German flag until 1861 when the ship was sold to Swedish owners.

On Margarethe's trip, the Olbers carried 288 passengers, 277 of them "Aliens," or German. Most of them gave St. Louis as their "Country of Allegiance," basically their intended destination. There were few cabin passengers on this trip; most of the passengers, like Margarethe and Friedrich, traveled steerage.

The journey from Bremen to America took about a month. Although a doctor was required for each immigrant ship, the voyage could be deadly, especially under crowded conditions. During Margarethe's trip, two infants on the ship died.

The prominence of New Orleans as a commercial center in the pre-Civil War era made New Orleans a prime destination for the immigrant trade. Ships unloaded their human cargos and reloaded cotton and other agricultural products for the return trip, products destined for trade centers in Europe. The attraction of the Port of New Orleans was further enhanced by the availability of steamboat travel up and down the Mississippi River. Steamboats floated the waters of the Mississippi, delivering immigrants into the American heartland. Boats going upstream from New Orleans took passengers deep into the Mississippi Valley. Produce brought back from the interior added to the exports available for the return trip to Europe.

During the antebellum period, New Orleans was the second leading port of entry in the United States behind only New York in drawing immigrants to its harbor. Between 1847 and 1857, approximately 350,000 immigrants arrived at New Orleans. Margarethe arrived during its peak years.

Adding to the hardship of the long journey to America, Margarethe was seven months pregnant. Two months after her arrival in New Orleans, a daughter named Sophie was born. The Ewe family was by this time settled in St. Louis, Missouri, where they rented an apartment next door to Margarethe's sister, Sophia, and her husband Henry Rauch. The two families were recorded in the 1860 census in June living in Ward Three of the City of St. Louis:[5] Friedrich was a tailor and Margarethe worked as a seamstress.

The 1860 census presented a genealogical puzzle. The Ewe family was entered under the surname "Ava"—"Friedrich, Margaret, and Sophia Ava." At the same time in the census enumeration, the name Rauch became "Henry and Sophia Rach."

Census takers often used phonetic spellings of names, which add to the difficulty of locating individuals in the census records, particularly if the names are of foreign origin. It is perhaps easy to understand how Rauch could be misspelled Rach. However, at first glance, one is hard pressed to see how the name Friedrich Ewe could become Friedrich Ava; that is, until German pronunciations are taken into consideration. In German the letter 'w' is pronounced as 'v' while 'e' is never sounded as the English 'e', rather generally as a variation of 'a'.

The Ewe family genealogy contains another conundrum. On January 18, 1861, Friedrich and Margarethe married in St. Louis. Margarethe used her maiden name Ficke and not Ewe.[6] The reason for this marriage is unknown. The couple immigrated as Friedrich and Margarethe Ewe. It is possible that they were not yet married when they came to America, notwithstanding the anticipated arrival of baby Sophie. Another explanation of a second marriage ceremony is that their German marriage had no legal status in the United States and rather than attempt to document their foreign vows, they simply exchanged them again in St. Louis.

Margarethe was 24 at the time of her arrival in America; Friedrich was 26. On the Olbers passenger manifest, Friedrich gave an occupation of "tailor" which he confirmed in the 1860 census. We may assume that he was working in that trade somewhere within St. Louis from 1859 to 1861. Unfortunately, nothing is known of him after 1861. Whether he was caught up in the opening events of the Civil War in St. Louis, died or was killed, or simply decided to return to Germany we do not know. Likewise, we do not know what happened to baby Sophie. She disappears from records about the same time. After a relatively rapid sequence of unknown events, Margarethe was alone.

Two years after her St. Louis marriage to Friedrich Ewe, single but retaining her married name of Margarethe Ficke Ewe, she married Henry Schaumann. They married in St. Louis before the justice of the peace on the 12th day of January 1863.[7]

One may only speculate about how Henry Schaumann and Margarethe met. They were both German immigrants, and each came from Hanover although from different cities some distance apart. It is unlikely that they knew each other in Germany, and probably met for the first time in St. Louis. The difference in their ages adds to the doubt that they were acquainted in Germany. When Henry emigrated probably around 1850 at about age 24, Margarethe was still a teenager of fourteen.

The Schaumann couple started their home in the Third Ward of St. Louis, in the same neighborhood as Henry and Sophia Rauch. Henry Schaumann is known to have lived in the Third Ward since at least 1860. It is probable that Margarethe met him there possibly through work connections to Henry Rauch. Henry's job as a mechanic, which he gave as his occupation on his Civil War enlistment papers in 1861, suggested a possible tie to Henry Rauch who worked in the construction business. In any event, it is conceivable that Henry and Margarethe met through common friendships with Sophia and Henry Rauch. By the time Margarethe and Henry married, Henry had secured a modest Civil War pension for his wartime disability. His employment options appear to have been limited because of his injury. Margarethe moved in with Henry and the couple set up housekeeping on South Third Street where Henry lived. Notwithstanding the hardships and uncertainties of the war years, they began their family. Friedrich Henry was born

November 21, 1863. Henry, Sr., was age 37; Margarethe 27 when he was born. Three years later, in August of 1866, Henry, Sr., died in the St. Louis cholera epidemic, leaving Margarethe with a three-year-old son to raise. He was baptized on a Sunday, December 9, 1866, at the Evangelical St. Marcus Church by the Rev. George W. Wall. Among the sponsors was little Henry's aunt, Sophia Rauch. The other sponsor Henry Rauch was not able to be present for the ceremony.[8]

We do not know how mother and child survived the cholera epidemic that took Henry's life, or how she managed to meet her needs. Henry and Sophia Rauch no doubt helped to look after her and her baby son. Margarethe was educated and possessed skills that would have been in demand during the war. We know, however, that her hope for a Civil War pension for young Henry as the son of a Civil War veteran never materialized despite efforts that lasted over a period of 34 years.

The Bremen Ship Olbers. Margarethe Ficke sailed to America aboard this ship in 1859. Anonymous painting dating from the 1850s. Oil on canvas, 22" x 32.3". Focke-Musuem. J. Lachs, *Schiffe aus Bremen; Bilder und Modelle im Focke-Museum*, 1994.

Concourse of the North German Lloyd Shipping Company at Bremerhaven in 1870. Cargo and passengers were loaded at this location. The North Germany Lloyd Company ran emigration and cargo routes from Bremerhaven to New York, Baltimore, and New Orleans. Historisches Museum Bremerhaven.

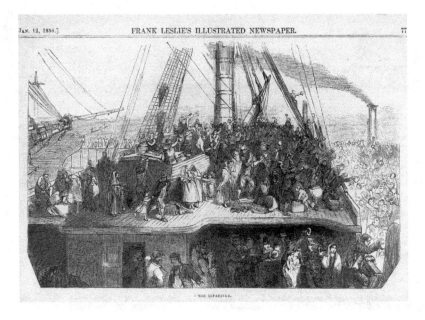

The Departure. Immigrants wave farewell to a crowd on the dock as their ship leaves Bremerhaven in 1856. The crowded conditions pictured in this wood engraving were typical of many ships that crossed the Atlantic. *Frank Leslie's Illustrated Newspaper*, Vol. 1 No. 5, January 12, 1856, p. 77. Library of Congress.

Passenger Manifest Page of the Bremen Ship Olbers. This report was filed by the ship's master on June 11, 1859, at the Port of New Orleans. On board were passengers number 100 and 101, Margarethe and Friedr' Ewe (arrows). New Orleans Passenger Lists, 1 Jan 1859 - 27 Jul 1859, National Archives and Records Administration.

New Orleans in 1852. This scene of New Orleans from St. Patrick's Church presents a view of the harbor and Mississippi River in the distance. Lithograph by B.F. Smith, Jr. Library of Congress.

New Orleans Steamboats of 1853. Immigrants who landed at the Port of New Orleans boarded steamboats like these tied up at the Sugar Levee to travel upstream to St. Louis and other Mississippi Valley destinations. Painting by Hippolyte Sebron, 1853. Oil on canvas, 48.5" x 72.3." Tulane University of Louisiana.

Friedrich Ewe and Margarethe Ficke Marriage Record. Missouri, County Marriage, Naturalization, and Court Records, 1800-1991, St. Louis Marriage Records 1860-1865 Vol. 10-11, image 154, Missouri State Archives, Jefferson City.

Marriage Record of Henry Schaumann and Margarethe Ficke Ewe. Their civil ceremony occurred on January 11, 1863, before Justice of the Peace Julius F. Schneider and was recorded on February 27, 1863 (arrow). Missouri, County Marriage, Naturalization, and Court Records, 1800-1991, Marriage Records of St. Louis County, 1806-1965 Vol. 10-11, image 464, Missouri State Archives, Jefferson City.

12

Trials of Trying Times

Margarethe married a third time, this time to Martin Zinner, a laborer and teamster by trade who drove for a St. Louis brewery company. Little is known about Zinner or the years that he and Margarethe spent together, except that they were brief.

Zinner came from Poppenreuth, Bavaria, Germany, a small town northwest of Nuremberg on the outskirts of Fürth. He was about five feet eight inches tall of dark complexion with brown eyes and hair. He was a Civil War veteran who enlisted for two tours in the Union army. On April 30, 1861, at the age of 27 he enrolled as a private in Company D of the Third Infantry Regiment of Missouri Volunteers.[1] He was among the first to answer President Abraham Lincoln's call for volunteers to put down the rebellion of the South following the attack on Fort Sumter. Missouri Governor Claiborne Jackson rebuffed Lincoln's order for troops and refused to send a single man into federal service. Senator Frank Blair in collusion with General Nathaniel Lyon (at that time Captain Lyon) offered to furnish Missouri's quota of volunteers, which Lincoln accepted. Beginning in April, men, almost entirely Germans, poured into the St. Louis Arsenal to enlist in Lyon's army. In a matter of days five regiments were formed. Colonel Franz Sigel commanded the Third Regiment. Zinner doubtless participated in Lyon's raid on Camp Jackson, a Missouri militia training camp set up on the edge of St. Louis. Union regiments surrounded the camp and demanded it surrender to Union forces. Southern partisans in the crowd fired shots into the Union ranks, and the soldiers returned fire. Dozens of innocent bystanders—men, women and children—died in what became infamously known as the St. Louis massacre.

On September 18, 1862, Pvt. Zinner re-enlisted, this time in Battery A of the Second Regiment Missouri Light Artillery. This was the unit of Henry Schaumann. Zinner's service period overlapped that of Henry's. They would have been together at Fort Wyman, in Rolla. He would have known of Henry's accident that led to Henry's disability discharge. Zinner served until August 1863.[2]

Martin Zinner and Margarethe married on April 6, 1867, seven and a half months after the death of Henry Schaumann.[3] This union produced a daughter Louise, born December 8, 1868.[4]

Sometime between March 1868 and April 1870, Martin Zinner was killed in an accident involving a runaway brewery wagon.[5] Margarethe was again suddenly a widow, this time with two small children, Henry age six, and Louise 18 months.

Margarethe and the children moved in with Henry and Sophia Rauch at their home in the Third Ward of St. Louis. Little Henry Schaumann took the surname Zinner and was known as Henry Zinner for at least a part of his childhood.

Margarethe worked as a seamstress in this period. Henry Rauch changed occupations and worked as a wood teamster. Sophia Rauch looked after chores at home.[6]

It is not known how long Margarethe and the children lived with the Rauchs. Henry Rauch's name appears frequently throughout the years as a witness on Margarethe's various marriage records and on documents submitted to the Civil War Pension Office on Margarethe's behalf. We may believe that the two families were never far apart. Sophia and Henry Rauch had no children and probably delighted in helping to raise Louise and Henry.

On May 29, 1871, Margarethe married Andreas Edelmann, Jr., a 36-year-old stone mason, according to census records, from the town of Schöningen, in the duchy of Brunswick, in old Hanover (now Lower Saxony), Germany. The town is on the southeastern rim of the Elm Hill Range, located near Brunswick, which in turn is on the navigational headwaters of the Oker River, which flows to the North Sea. Schöningen became famous of late as the home of the Schöningen Spears, an archaeology discovery of the worlds oldest manufactured wooden weapons dating back approximately 400,000 years.

Edelmann immigrated to America aboard the ship Hermann, sailing out of Bremen, traveling in steerage, and listed on the ship's manifest as a farmer. He arrived at the Port of New York on January 4, 1865.[7] He soon made his way to Missouri, married, and had a son named William, eventually convincing his father Andreas, a brother William and his sister Lottie to join him in St. Louis.[8]

When Margarethe and Andreas married in 1871, it was his second marriage and Margarethe's fourth. On the record of their marriage, she did not bother to include any of her previous marriages to Ewe, Schaumann, and Zinner, electing instead to use as her surname "Dothier," an obvious alliteration to her middle name Dorothea and a confounder to future genealogists.[9]

The Edelmann family settled into a place on South Third Street near the Rauch family. By 1880 the Edelmann blended family included Andreas, Margarethe, Henry Schaumann, William Edelmann, Louise Zinner, and Andreas Edelmann, Sr., the 74-year-old father of Andreas, all living under the surname Edelmann.

The 1880 census was taken twice in St. Louis. From the first enumeration in the middle of June to the time it was enumerated again in November, Friedrich Henry Schaumann, who was age 17 in 1880, changed jobs from being a stone mason like his step-father to working in a tobacco warehouse, a first step to going out on his own.[10]

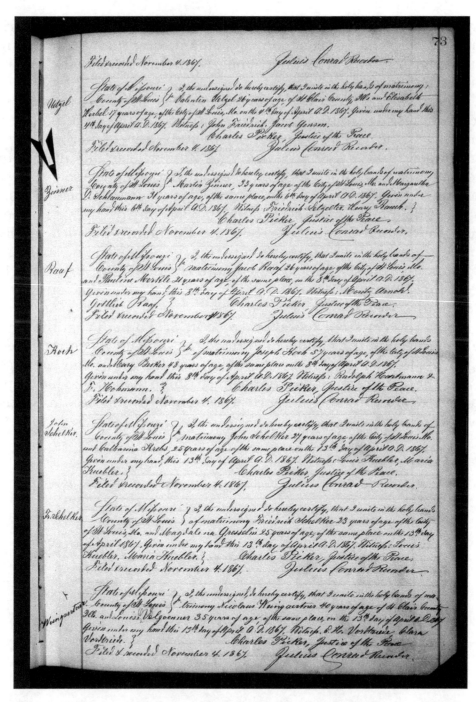

Martin Zinner and Margarethe D. Schaumann Marriage Record. Missouri, County Marriage, Naturalization, and Court Records, 1800-1991, Marriage Records of St. Louis and St. Louis Co., 1806-1965, Vol. 12-13 1865-1869, p. 73, image 471, Index image 433. Missouri State Archives.

Andreas Edelmann and Margarethe "Dothier" Marriage Record. Missouri, County Marriage, Naturalization, and Court Records, 1800-1991, St. Louis and St. Louis Co., 1806-1965, Vol. 15, 1868-1873, p. 54, image 463; St. Louis Marriage records index 1871-1881 male image 100, Missouri State Archives, Jefferson City.

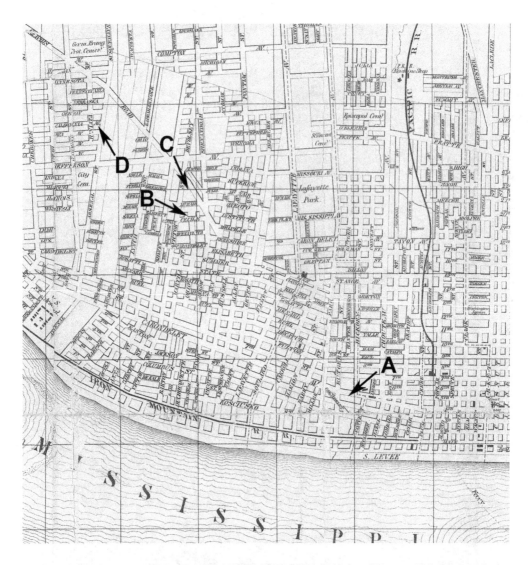

St. Louis Addresses of Margarethe Ficke Ewe Schaumann Zinner Edelmann from 1863 to 1900. (A) 1259 South Third Street; (B) 2316 Cecile Street; (C) 2204 Gravois Avenue; and (D) 3108 California Avenue. Margarethe's son, Henry Schaumann, lived at the 3108 California Avenue address. Margarethe also used that address as a postal address in her widow's pension application. US Census and Soldier's Service Record and Pension File. National Archives. Map adapted from Kennedy's Sectional Map of St. Louis, 1859. St. Louis Public Library.

City of St. Louis in 1872. In this view across the Mississippi River, Eads Bridge under construction is seen in the distance. The bridge opened in 1874. Wood engraving by A.C. Warren and R. Hinshelwood, 1872. Library of Congress.

Margarethe Dorothea Edelmann. Signed Margarethe D. Schaumann
from Henry Schaumann widow's pension claim. National Archives
and Records Administration.

13

The House at Billings

For many years after the Civil War ended, St. Louis never fully settled its political differences. The Germans were held responsible—and accepted that responsibility—for keeping Missouri in the Union. Southern partisans in and around St. Louis harbored an ethnic bias against Germans that never went away.

Henry and Sophia Rauch left St. Louis in 1882 and settled on an 80-acre parcel of land in North Polk Township, Christian County, Missouri, in a fertile agricultural region of southwest Missouri, near the little town of Billings. Soon after, Andreas Edelmann began a process to move his family out of St. Louis, too.[1] He picked a site on the Rauch property near the Rauch family and built a house with materials salvaged from buildings in St. Louis and transported by the Frisco Railroad to the depot at Billings.[2] The materials went from there by horse and wagon to the farm site three and a quarter miles northwest of town.

According to family tradition, "They built a 3-room house for staying in the summer. Grandpa Edelmann, who was a stonemason, used parts of demolished buildings from St. Louis. To build the summer place, he fired his own brick on the site for insulation in the foot-thick walls. The original room partitions in the house were curtains."[3]

For a couple of years the family divided their time between their country place at Billings and their home in St. Louis, before deciding to leave St. Louis for good to make their permanent home on the farm at Billings. They adopted a baby daughter and named her Rosina. Margarethe filled the role of mother and homemaker; Andreas farmed and worked in Billings. He took time to found the Lutheran Church, in Billings.[4]

"They moved from St. Louis to the farm near Billings, Missouri, in 1884 and built a home on their farm," the tradition continues. "Mr. Edelmann and his stepson Henry Schaumann were brick masons by trade. They farmed the 80-acre farm and did masonry work in Billings and surrounding areas. Henry Schaumann married Agnes Arnold in 1901 and moved into the same house with Mr. and Mrs. Andrew Edelmann. The original house was one long room with a full basement and an outside stairway leading to the upper floor that served as bedrooms. After Henry and Agnes Schaumann were married, additions were built on to the house including a large living room and two large bedrooms, an upstairs attic and a third story bedroom and attic."

As often happens in life stories, tragedy again entered. Sophia Rauch, Margarethe's beloved sister of so many years, committed suicide after her husband Henry Rauch died. She came to the Edelmann home and in the southeast corner of the house drank a deadly chemical that ended her life.[5]

In the 1900 US Census, enumerators were given additional questions to ask that substantially expanded the amount of information about each person. It confirmed many of the details of Andreas and Margarethe Edelmann's lives.[6] However, it was not until the 1910 US Census that new information came to light. Perhaps due partly to memory, and partly to a census taker's error, Margarethe gave her number of marriages as two instead of four, which may be easily dismissed as a clerical error. However, when asked the mother of how many children, living and deceased, she said five and two still living.[7] This was different from her answer to a similar question on the 1900 census when she said three children and two living. In that census, son Henry Schumann and daughter Louise Zinner would be the two living; the deceased would be Sophie Ewe, her assumed firstborn. When the number increased to five total and two living, the mystery deepened. Two children were unaccounted for. A sometimes-discounted family tradition says that there was a child born to Friedrich Ewe and Margarethe in Germany but died before their emigration to America. More plausible perhaps was a story remembered by her grandson, Arthur, "Dad's mother had two children by Schaumann. Dad and a sister who was killed by being kicked in the head by a horse." Others remembered that it was a child of Mr. Edelmann by his first marriage who was killed.[8] Meanwhile, Tucked away in the St. Louis Death Register of 1866 is an entry dated January 14,

1866, for "Mrs. Schoenmanns Child, stillborn, buried in Holy Ghost Cemetery." Henry Schaumann died in August 1866 and was also buried in Holy Ghost Cemetery. Their graves were later moved and lost.

Andreas Edelmann died on December 6, 1919, at the age of 84. Margarethe lived to the ripe old age of 93. She died October 26, 1929. She was buried in Rose Hill Cemetery, Christian County, Missouri, beside Andreas her husband of 48 years six months and seven days. Dr. Fred Brown attributed her death to senility. Services were in the German Evangelical Church under Rev. F.W. Weltze.[9]

Henry Schaumann and Agnes Arnold went on to have four daughters and one son: Margaret, Rosenia, Louise, Henrietta, and Arthur, all grandchildren of Henry and Margarethe Schaumann.

The son, Arthur Schaumann, grandson of Henry and Margarethe, married Valentine Kastendieck in 1940. They made their home at the original Edelmann residence. Arthur purchased an additional 40 acres in 1944 making the home place a total of 120 acres. In 1948, porches and a bathroom were added to the home. A new chimney was constructed and a wood-burning furnace was placed in the basement. A utility room was added.[10]

"Billings, Missouri, May 8, 1947.

"Dear Uncle Albert and Aunt Mary.[11]

"Are you glad that spring is here again? We are very glad to have it warm again, especially Jayme Sue. She loves to play out in the sunshine, which is very good for her. She has had one or two bad colds this past winter. I believe Henrietta has written to you mentioning that the Schaumann Mortgage would probably be paid to you soon. We are ready to pay you anytime and we were wondering just how you would like for us to send it. We can mail you a check or pay it at the bank or just anyway that you would like for us to do it. You can let us know. Arthur and I are buying the farm from his mother and we would like to pay what is owed to you, first. Mother Schaumann and Henrietta have a nice place selected that they wish to buy. It is a nice rock house and garage with chicken house and ten acres of pasture, all of which will be a suitable 'set-up' and is located near town, so Henrietta wouldn't have far to go to work. Farming has been favorable the past few years; of course, we don't know just when a 'slump' might come. We are now milking ten cows and with the good spring pasture, they are giving lots of milk. That is our main farming project, but I'm planning on having chickens next year. I have been teaching school but intend to stay home for a few years now. Jayme needs her mother and I can do so much more work here. The rural and small town school teachers still don't get a very high salary. If I should teach again I would return to college for one summer and get my degree and then I know the salary would be better.

"We hope you are well. We are all feeling quite well at the present. We would have liked to come to Kansas City, but with our other expenses we thought we could do our business by mail if that is satisfactory to you. If you will let us know how you want the payment we will act accordingly.

"Love,

"Arthur, Valentine & Jayme"

Death Register for Infant of Margrethe and Henry Schaumann. This entry (pointer) in the St. Louis Register of Deaths records the stillbirth of "Mrs. Schoenmanns Child" on January 14, 1866. The baby was buried in Holy Ghost Cemetery. St. Louis (Independent City) Vital Records, Register of Deaths, 1850-1909, Vol. 1, January 1866 - October 1867, p. 11, image 22. Missouri State Archives.

Andreas Edelmann. Signature from Henry Schaumann minor's pension claim. National Archives and Records Administration.

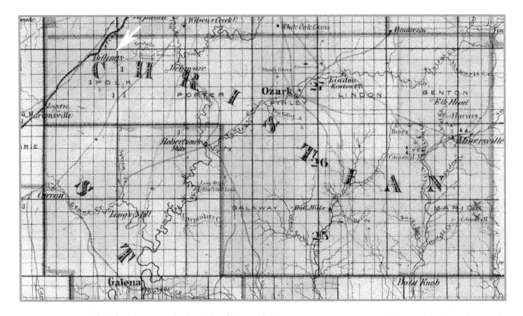

Map of Christian County, Missouri. Margarethe and Andreas Edelmann settled in North Polk Township at the extreme western end of the panhandle of Christian County. This 1874 map was drawn a decade and a half after the county's organization in 1859. The town of Billings is shown in the upper left corner situated on the Atlantic and Pacific (Frisco) Railroad. *Campbell's New Atlas of Missouri*, 1874. Springfield-Greene County Library.

A Busy Day in Billings. Billings, Missouri, was a flourishing town when Margarethe and Andreas Edelmann moved to Christian County from St. Louis in 1884. Market days and fair events drew large crowds from the farms that made up the larger community of Billings. Undated photo, Author's Collection.

Frisco Steam Locomotive. The Edelman family arrived in Billings aboard a passenger train pulled by a steam locomotive similar to this Manchester engine built in 1880. Passenger service into southwest Missouri was relatively new when the Edelmanns came to Christian County in 1884. Frisco Archives, Springfield-Greene County Library.

The J.W. Sanders Mercantile Building on Elm Street, Billings, Missouri. From a small beginning the Sanders Mercantile Company grew to be one of the flourishing enterprises in southwest Missouri. It later became the J.B. Berghaus Mercantile. The Bank of Billings first opened for business in part of this building on May 14, 1889. Collection of the Bank of Billings.

Friedrich Henry Schaumann. Signature from Civil War minor's pension claim. National Archives and Records Administration.

14

The Civil War Pension System

W hen Henry Schaumann died he left a widow and small son without any visible means of a livelihood. Margarethe sought to claim a widow's pension, which was essentially a continuation of the disability pension Henry drew because of his injury during the Civil War. The military pension office denied her claim because, among other things, his death was not caused by military action. Thus began a squabble with the US Government that lasted for decades. The story of this impasse opens a window on a bureaucratic morass that had a profound impact on the lives of Henry's descendants that was still being discussed years after his death. Because of the central part it played, the case is presented in detail to show where the government's decision to deny a pension claim was wrong and where Margarethe's arguments were correct from the beginning.[1] As Henry's grandson used to say, "It was an unfair treatment because no one got a dime out of it."

The administration of the veterans' pension system is as old as the country. The disabled veteran pension system was first adopted by the colonies on August 26, 1776. After the establishment of the federal government in 1789, some states refused to pay for pensions, and administration of pensions was transferred to the federal level under the supervision of the Secretary of War. By the Act of March 3, 1849, the pension process passed from the War Department to the Department of Interior in which was established the Pension Office, which became a bureau of that department under the supervision of the Secretary of Interior. Because of fraudulent claims, regional offices were created to avoid the accumulation of cases and to facilitate the process of verifying information. By the time of the Civil War, the Pension Office was a large bureaucracy responsible for veterans of the War of 1812, the US-Mexican War, and the Indian Wars, with agencies in many states.

A significant legacy of the US Civil War was the expansion of the country's military pension system. Out of the 2.7 million men who enlisted in the Union Army, 2.4 million survived the war. The war thus produced a large number of wounded or otherwise disabled veterans who might claim reward for their service. In addition, there were widows and other dependents of soldiers who had died in the war who were allowed to claim a pension. Throughout the war and afterwards from the Reconstruction period through the early 20th Century, Congress continually modified the Union Army pension legislation, making it more flexible and generous. The political maneuvering of the major political parties used pension legislation as a strategy to recruit voters. The northern politicians in particular were eager to reward veterans with pensions from a windfall of money because of the Civil War and the heavy tariffs that had been exacted.

The General Law Pension System Act of July 22, 1861, was initially implemented to authorize pensions to Civil War veterans with war-related disabilities only and for widows and orphans of deceased soldiers. Then, on July 14, 1862, this law was updated to provide pensions for soldiers who suffered permanent bodily injury or had any disability as a direct consequence of military duty, not necessarily battle-related. The General Law system granted pensions to widows or, if there was no widow, to the children under 16 years of age of any person deceased after March 4, 1861, because of any wound or disease contracted while in the service. The pension to widows and minors was the same as would have been allowed to the husband or father for total disability, about $8 per month for total disability for enlisted personnel, more for officers. Subsequent legislation gradually increased the amount of pension for widows and dependents, concluding with the Act of July 3, 1926, when Civil War widows and dependents could receive up to $50 per month. Under the General Law, a widow or dependent relative could not be pensioned unless the cause of the soldier's death originated in service in the line of duty. Upon the death or remarriage of the widow, the minor children of the soldier if under the age of 16 years became entitled to the pension.

With the passage of the Arrears Act of January 25, 1879, veterans and their dependents were permitted to collect, in addition to a monthly pension, a lump sum payment based on the date of death or discharge from service. The Arrears Law was approved thanks mainly to the efforts of the claims agents and lawyers who tried to make the process of pension application more attractive to veterans and widows. With the approval of the Arrears Law, pensions were granted from the date either of death or of discharge from service and not from the date of filing of the pension application, as was previously the case.

The other major source for the expansion of the pension system was the Disability Act of 1890, which allowed for pensions based only on time of service, without regard to the existence of war-related disabilities. In contrast to the General Law system, the Act of June 27, 1890, was a service-based system. The pension was provided based on proof of at least 90 days of military service in the Civil War, of having been honorably discharged, and of the existence of a bodily disability not caused by vicious habits but not necessarily of service origin. Pensions were also given to the widows and children of Civil War soldiers without regard to the cause of the soldier's death. The pension commenced from the date of filing the application after the passage of this Act, and with the proof that the disability existed. Application for a pension could be under the General Law or the Disability Law but not both.

Before 1890, a widow was only eligible for a pension if she could prove that her husband's death was war-related. After 1890, the widows of those who served 90 days or more in the Civil War were entitled to be pensioned at the rate of $8 per month, without regard to the cause of the soldier's death. Widows became entitled under the law if they married the soldier prior to 27 June 1890, provided they were without means of support other than their daily labor, and an actual net income not exceeding $250 per year, and had not remarried. Claims of children under 16 years of age were governed by the same conditions as applied to widows, except that their dependence was presumed and need not be shown by evidence.

The application process could be tedious. For that reason, veterans and their dependents often hired pension attorneys, or agents. Through the application process, the Bureau of Pensions' practice allowed veterans to hire lawyers to shepherd their cases. Lawyers played a significant role in the increasing number of applications for pensions as each new pension law was enacted. Some law firms at the end of the 19th Century specialized in military pensions, with attorneys traveling around the country drumming up people eligible for pensions. The approval of the Arrears Act and Act of 1890 served as important incentives for lawyers to intervene in the pension application process. The complexity of many cases and the large number of veterans who sought legal assistance empowered veterans in their dealing with the Pension Office because lawyers tried to sustain their client's claims, solicit independent medical opinions for clients who were rejected by the bureau's medical board, and pursue appeals. Lawyers were paid only if successful. Legislation also fixed the compensation that attorneys should receive to $10 per successful claim in order to protect veterans.

The regional claims office received the claims from veterans for a pension. Once the claim for adjudication was received in any pension office, it was assigned to one of the examiners who was in charge of the process. The first thing the examiner did in order to adjudicate a claim was to determine whether the declaration was properly executed and sufficient to its allegations. He then asked the War Department for a report showing the full military history of the soldier and his hospital treatment. If there was no clear evidence of the origin in the line of duty or existence in service from the files of the War Department, the claimant was required to establish these points by the testimony of officers or comrades having personal knowledge of the facts. They were required to set out all the circumstances in which the disability was incurred. After receiving this evidence, the Adjutant General of the US Army was asked for a report showing whether the people who testified were present at the time and place their affidavits had referenced. An order was then sent to the claimant or to his attorney if he had one, for the claimant to appear for examination before a board of United States examining surgeons at a location near his or her place of residence.

The boards of surgeons were instructed to confirm that the veterans' medical conditions were genuine and to rate the severity of disabilities. During the examination, surgeons were to evaluate what disability, if any, existed, the degree to which the disability rendered the applicant unable to perform manual labor, whether or not the disability was a consequence of military service on the basis of the soldier's history given to him, the probable duration of the disability, and how the habits of the applicant affected the origin and continued duration of the disability. The members of the surgeons' board were to be in attendance during all pension examinations. Any knowledge by a member of the board indicating that the disability evaluated was caused or exacerbated by an injury or accident out of service, or by the claimant's own vicious habits, was to be noted. The board was also required to note questionable claims, and to issue an opinion regarding the validity of claims. After each examination, the board generated a surgeons' certificate. Every certificate had information about the physical condition of the pensioner at the date of the examination. The surgeons had to describe and rate separately everything they found. The certificate also had information about the rate of respiration per minute, pulse and the weight of the patient. These certificates remained as a permanent record of the claimant's medical history. The surgeons were to determine the degree of disability, but ultimately it was the law and the Pension Bureau that fixed the sum of money to be paid for each degree of disability. If the claim was based upon a disability arising from a disease contracted in service, the Pension Office accepted the veteran's claim and rated the disability based on the surgeon's certificate. In the opposite case, if the board of surgeons reported no evidence of the existence of disability from the cause or causes alleged, the claimant was advised of this fact and had the opportunity to find evidence showing that he was in some degree incapacitated for the performance of manual labor due to such cause. For that purpose, the claim was held open for about 100 days, at which time the pension application was rejected if no other evidence was shown.

Veterans whose claims were rejected or whose requests for pension increases were denied received notice from the Bureau of Pensions and had twelve months to supply the evidence needed to sustain the claim. Upon re-submission, a Bureau examiner would prepare a brief to summarize the facts of the case, assess the weight and character of the evidence, and decide whether the claim should be accepted or rejected. A Review Board considered the brief with rules that specified that questions of fact were the province of the examiner who prepared the brief and that the sole function of the Review Board was to treat cases judicially based upon the papers. After considering the papers, the Review Board solicited an opinion on the medical evidence in the case from a medical reviewer. If it was sustained the claim was accepted.

Civil War Pension Cards of Henry Schaumann. Compiled Service Records of Volunteer Union Soldiers Who Served in Organizations from the State of Missouri, microfilm M405 roll 340, Second Light Artillery, Ru-Sch, National Archives and Records Administration.

15

Disability Discharge of Henry Schaumann

Henry Schaumann was injured during the Civil War in early October of 1862 while Company A of the 2nd Regiment Light Artillery was encamped along the Pacific Railroad at a place between Rolla and Ft. Wyman, Missouri. He was honorably discharged in November 1862. The next year he was given a disability pension, but when he died in 1866, his wife and young son were denied survivor pension benefits.

Documents in the Henry Schaumann pension file have been ordered below by date to clarify the chronology of the record. Important dates in the life of Henry Schaumann have been inserted into the record to complete the chronology of his life during this time. Numbers in parentheses ( ) identify the order of original documents in the pension file available at the National Archives and Records Administration, Washington, D.C.[1] Most of the information contained in the original documents is handwritten. Where writing is illegible, missing, or terms are uncertain, these are indicated with [ ] in the transcription. The symbol /s/ denotes a signature. Spelling and abbreviations are as they appear in the documents. Transcriber's comments are in italics.

Documents in Order of Their Dates

14 Oct 1861. Henry Schaumann enlists at St. Louis, Missouri, in Capt. Laux's Company, A, 2nd Reg. Light Artillery, Missouri Volunteers, Union Army.

1 Oct 1862. Injured while on duty at a place on the Pacific Railroad between Rolla and Ft. Wyman, Missouri.

22 Oct 1862. Femoral Hernia diagnosed. *Note: A femoral hernia is a loop of intestine, or another part of the abdominal contents, that has been forced out of the abdomen through a channel called the "femoral canal", a tube-shaped passage at the top of the front of the thigh. About the size of a grape, a femoral hernia can cause serious medical problems if left untreated, even if there are no troublesome symptoms to begin with.*

31 Oct 1862 (1) Certificate of Disability for Discharge. Henry Schaumann private of Captain M. [Michael] Laux Company A of the Second Artillery Regiment of United States Mo. Volunteers, was enlisted by Captain M. Laux, of the Second Regiment of Mo. Artillery at St. Louis on the 14th day of October 1861, to serve 3 years; he was born in Hildesheim in the State of Hanover, is thirty-seven years of age, 5 feet 6 ½ inches high, dark complexion, grey eyes, dark hair, and by occupation when enlisted a Mechanic. During the last two months said soldier has been unfit for duty [no entry] days. Said private Schaumann has a rupture on the right side, which showed itself on the 22d day of October 1862 at Rolla Mo. but which was produced about the first of October (while camping on the Rail Road between Rolla and Fort Wyman) while carrying water for washing and drinking purposes and in the service by falling into a hollow at said Rail Road accidentally. Station: Fort Wyman near Rolla, Mo. Date: October 31, 1862. /s/ Charles Faist, 1st Lieut. Commanding Company.

I certify, that I have carefully examined the said Henry Schaumann of Captain Laux's Company, and find him incapable of performing the duties of a soldier because of Femoral Hernia of the right side received by accidentally falling into a ditch in the month of October 1862, which injury disables him in my opinion one-half from obtaining his subsistence by manual labor. /s/ J.B. Condrove, Surgeon 2d Reg. Mo. Art.

22 Nov 1862. (2) Discharge Approval. Headquarters, Department of the Missouri, St. Louis. Discharge approved by order of Major General Curtis.

15. Disability Discharge of Henry Schaumann

24 Nov 1862. (1) Disability Discharge. Discharged this twenty fourth day of November 1862, at Rolla, Mo. /s/ Harry Graham, Lt. Col., Commanding the Post. *Note: Henry Schaumann's name subsequently appeared on a Detachment Muster-out Roll, Benton Barracks, [St. Louis], May 24, 1863. Discharged for disability on surgeon's certificate Nov 24/62. /s/ [?] copyist.*

16 Dec 1862 (3) Medical Examination. St. Louis. Examining Surgeon's Certificate. I hereby certify, that I have carefully examined Henry Schaumann, late a Private, Co A, 2d Mo Artillery in the service of the United States, who was discharged at [no entry], on the [ ] day of [no entry] 186[ ], and is an applicant for an invalid pension, by reason of alleged disability resulting from Femoral Hernia. In my opinion the said Henry Schaumann is one-half incapacitated for obtaining his subsistence by manual labor from the cause above stated. Judging from his present condition, and from the evidence before me, it is my belief that the said disability arose in the service aforesaid in the line of duty. The disability is of a permanent character. A more particular description of the applicant's condition is subjoined: Femoral Hernia of right side. Occasioned by a fall - Oct 1st 1862. His disability is likely to be permanent unless surgical means of relief are resorted to. /s/ J. B. Colegrove, Examining Surgeon

26 Dec 1862 (2) Discharge is officially recorded in the Adjutant General's Office.

12 Jan 1863(17) Henry Schaumann marries Margarethe Ficke Ewe. *Note: See 11 Oct 1866 for certified copy of marriage certificate.*

16

Application for an Invalid Pension

The following papers (8-14) document Henry Schaumann's successful application for a disability pension.

2 Feb 1863 (8) Application for Invalid Pension. State of Missouri. County of St. Louis. On this second day of February A.D. 1862 [*sic*] personally appeared before me, the undersigned Clerk of the St. Louis Circuit Court in the State of Missouri, Henry Schaumann, 37 years of age, a resident of St. Louis Missouri, who being by me first duly sworn according to law, declares that he is the identical Henry Schaumann who enlisted in the United States service on the 14th day of October 1861, as a private in Captain Laux's Company A, 2d Regt. of Artillery Mo. Vols., Colonel Almstedt, for three years in the war against the rebels, and was honorably discharged the 24th October 1862 in Rolla [*actual date of discharge was 24 Nov 1862*], that in the service of aforesaid, and in the line of his duty, he received the following injury to wit: A rupture on the right side, which showed itself on the 22d day of October, 1862 at Rolla Mo. which he however contracted about the first day of October while camping on the Rail Road between Rolla and Fort Wyman, and carrying water for washing and drinking purposes by falling accidentally into a hollow near said Rail Road, that he has resided in St. Louis since leaving the service, that he is a mechanic by occupation, but by reason of said injury one-half disabled from obtaining his subsistence by manual labor, reference is hereby made to the official report of the proper officer on file in the Adjutant General's Office in Washington, D.C., and the certificate of the examining surgeon of the Pension

Department forwarded by him to your Department, that deponent has had no occupation since leaving the service and that he hereby constitutes and appoints Randolph Mackwitz of St. Louis, Mo. his attorney to prosecute this claim and to do all things necessary to obtain an invalid pension for him and to receive the same. Witness: /s/ H. Goetemann Witness: /s/ H. Rauch /s/ Heinrick Schaumann. And I the said Clerk of the St. Louis Circuit Court further certify, that at the same time personally appeared before me H. Goetemann and H. Rauch, residents of St. Louis Mo, persons whom I certify to be respectable and entitled to credit and who being by me duly sworn, say that they were present and saw Henry Schaumann sign his name to the foregoing declaration and they further swear that they have every reason to believe from the appearance of the applicant and their acquaintance with him that he is the identical person he represents himself to be, that the habits of the above claimant have been temperate and that he has had no occupation since leaving the service, that these deponents reside in the City of St. Louis, State aforesaid, and that they are wholly disinterested. Witness: /s/ Sam Mackwitz /s/ H. Goetemann /s/ H. Rauch. Certified by the Clerk with the note: St. Louis, Mo., to be advertised in the German paper. *Note: H. Rauch is listed as a witness on this application. Henry Rauch was the husband of Sophia Ficke Rauch, sister of Margarethe who was the wife of Henry Schaumann. Newly married to Margarethe, Henry Schaumann clearly was acquainted with the Rauch family.*

18 Feb 1863 (9) Testimony of Officer. Affidavit of Lt. Troll. I certify on honor that on or about the first day of October 1862 my Company was encamped near the Rail Road, between Rolla and Fort Wyman that private Henry Schaumann of my Company was ordered to fetch water from the springs, for the use of the Company and that while so employed he accidentally fell from the embankment of said Rail Road and injured himself which injury after examination on the 24th of October 1862 in Rolla by the regimental surgeon was found to be hernia on the right side, I further certify that the injury was received without any fault or negligence on the part of the said private Schaumann. St. Louis,

February 18th 1863 /s/ Henry Troll, 1 Lieut, Co A 2d Regd Arty. Mo. Vol.] *Note: This document, written in the hand of Lt. Troll, gives a date of 24 Oct, not 22, as the time of examination. Also, the commanding officer was Lt. Troll, not Laux as cited in other documents. Troll apparently replaced Laux as commander of Battery A in February 1862. See document 10 below.*

5 Aug 1863 (10) Certificate of the Commanding Officer. Headq. 2d Regt. Arty. Mo. Vols., St. Louis, Mo. I do hereby certify, that 1st Lieut. Henry Troll of Comp A 2d Regt Arty. Mo. Vols. acknowledges his signature to the within certificate, and that he is Jr. 1st lieut of Comp. A, 2d Regt. Arty. Mo. Vols. since February 23rd 1862, when he was commissioned as such by the Governor of the State of Missouri /s/ [not legible] Lt. Col. Cmdr. 2d Regt, Arty, Mo. Vols, Headquarters State of Mo., August 7, 1863. Witnessed by John B. Gray Adj. Gen. of Mo.

29 Aug 1863 (11) Summary Brief and Admittance to Pension. Claim for an Invalid Pension under Pension Act of 1862. Brief in the case of Henry Schaumann Private Company A, 2d Regiment Mo. Art.; Enlisted 14th October 1861. Discharged 24th Nov 1862. Post Office Address of Applicant: St. Louis (W.S. 3d St. Bet. Convent & Rugers Sts.), St. Louis Co. Mo. Proof Exhibited: Charles Faist-1st Lieut of Claimant's Co.--certifies that "he has a rupture on right side, which showed itself on 22d day of October 1862, at Rolla, Mo., but was produced about the 1st of said month (while camping on the Rail Road, between Rolla & Fort Wyman) while carrying water for washing and drinking purposes, and in the service, by falling into a hollow at said Rail Road accidentally." Army Surgeon states "Femoral hernia of the right side, received by accidentally falling into a ditch, in month of October 1862, which injury disables him, in my opinion, one-half, from obtaining his subsistence by manual labour." Examining Surg. Colegrove certifies "Femoral hernia of right side likely to be permanent unless surgical means of relief are resorted to. Disability one-half." Admitted Aug. 29th, 1863, to a pension of $4.00 per month, commencing November 24th, 1862. Disability: One-half. Disabled by Femoral

hernia, of right side. /s/ Rudolph Mackwitz, Esq, Agent St. Louis, Mo., /s/ W. R. Morriz, Examining Clerk

29 Aug 1863 (12) Records Jacket. Communication to Attorney. Act of July 14, 1862. War of 1861. Vol. 3, page 418. Henry Schaumann, St. Louis, Mo. Private Co A 2d Mo. Art. Discharged Oct. 24th, 1862. Admitted Aug 29, 1863 to a pension of $4 per month, Commencing November 24, 1862 /s/ W.R. Morris. Received Feb 24th, 1863. Rudolph [sic] Mackwitz, St. Louis, Mo., Attorney. *Note: An untitled page which accompanies the preceding communication appears to be an attempt on the part of the attorney to locate Mr. Schaumann on July 23, 1863, and again on July 30, 1863. Under the law, Henry would have received a lump sum payment of $36 at the rate of $4 per month from November 1862, the time of his discharge and $4 per month thereafter. Under the February 1862 agreement (8) Attorney Mackwitz was entitled to a fee of up to $10. The $4 per month pension was set by statute, being one-half of the maximum $8 allowed for a disability. A single hernia was allowed one-half.*

5 Sep 1863 (13) Records Jacket for Pension Papers. Invalid. Cert. No. 16,459 Henry **Schaumann**, Pri; Co. A-2-Mo. Vol Art. Original Roll: St. Louis. Issued Sept 5, 1863, Rate and period, $4, from Nov. 24, 1862. Disability: Femoral Hernia of right side. For endorsements see inside. *Note: Pension certificate No. 16,459 was later surrendered by Margarethe Schaumann, widow of Henry Schaumann.*

5 Sep 1863 (14) Record of Pension. Missouri. Henry Schaumann Rank: Private, Company: A, Regiment 2 Mo. Art. St. Louis Agency. Rate per month, $4, Commencing 24 Nov 1862. Certificate dated 5 Sept 1863 and sent to R. Mackwitz, St. Louis, Mo. Act of 14 July, 1862. Book F Vol 10 Page 136 /s/ signature, Clerk [Note]: Femoral hernia of right side.

21 Nov 1863 Birth of Frederick Henry Schaumann, in St. Louis.

20 Aug 1866 Henry Schaumann dies in St. Louis. *Note: This date conflicts with a burial certificate provided to the pension*

board giving 13 Nov 1867 as date of death See (13) Jul 1883. The 1867 certificate was apparently a case of mistaken identity.

17

Declaration of Guardianship

In less than four years after his disability discharge–and three years after the birth of his son, Henry Schaumann died. There followed a series of futile attempts by his widow, son, and other interested parties to claim a dependent pension based on his service record. As the documentation shows, attempts by the family of Henry Schaumann to establish pension rights beyond his death covered a period of 34 years, from 1866 until 1900 when the claims were finally abandoned.

8 Oct 1866 (16) Pension arrears paid to Dorothea Margarethe Schaumann, Guardian of Frederick Henry Schaumann. 11 Oct 1866 Notice to U.S. Pension Agency, St. Louis, Mo. Sir: The [not legible] certificate is [?]. He died on the 23d day of August 1866, and on the 8th Oct '66, his widow was paid the arrears due her deceased husband, the certificate being surrendered, which will be forwarded to Washington with the papers for this month. Respectfully /s/ A.C. Wood, Clerk copy to Francis Minor, Esq., St. Louis, Mo. *Note: This document has "paid" written across it. There is no indication of an amount of the payment, only an entry and date recording the payment. Pensions were paid quarterly on the fourth day of the month. It is important to point out that proof of death in August 1866 as well as verification of Margarethe as widow would have been required for payment to occur.*

11 Oct 1866 (17) Certified Copy of Marriage Record. State of Missouri. County of St. Louis. I certify that I have this twelfth day of January A.D. 1863 joined in the holy bonds of matrimony Mr. Henry Schaumann, late of Klauen, near

Peine, Hannover, now St. Louis Mo. & Mrs. Dorothea Margarethe Ewe, nee Ficke, late of St. Huelpe, Hannover, now of St. Louis. Mr. Jubill F. Lohneider, Justice of the Peace. Filed and Recorded February of 1863. A.C. Bernoudy, Recorder. State of Missouri. County of St. Louis. I the undersigned Recorder of Deeds in and for the County of St. Louis, do hereby certify that the foregoing is a true copy of the marriage certificate of Henry Schaumann & Dorothea Margarethe Ewe and of the date of filing & recording thereof as fully as the same remained of Record in my office in Marriage Record Book No. 11, page 82. Witness my hand & official seal of office this 11th day of October 1866. /s/ Julius Courad, Recorder. *Note: This record and the following acknowledgment, contained in the pension file of Henry Schaumann, clearly established Margarethe as the widow of Henry. Under the General Law system, the widow of a deceased veteran was entitled to the same pension that would have been allowed to the husband, provided she could show that her husband died of a war-related cause, and provided she had not remarried. This law applied to any person deceased after March 4, 1861, as a result of any wound or disease contracted while in the service. No record exists of Margarethe having applied for a widow's pension in 1866. Her efforts were focused on obtaining a minor's pension for her son, Friedrich Henry. It is an open question as to why she did not petition as a widow because her pension would have transferred automatically to her son Henry when she remarried.*

It is unclear why it was felt that the following documents were necessary. Margarethe was taking steps to legally establish herself as guardian of Frederick Henry. Henry, as a minor under age 16, was eligible for a pension benefit, except the law required at the time that the death of the service member must occur because of a war-related cause. This requirement was repealed in the Act of June 27, 1890, when a pension was provided based on proof of at least ninety days of military service in the Civil War, of having been honorably discharged, and of the existence of a bodily disability. Pensions were given to the widows and children of Civil War soldiers without regard to the cause of the soldier's death. Unfortunately, by 1890, Friedrich Henry, the son of Henry Schaumann, had passed the age 16-eligibility cutoff.

9 Dec 1866 (21) Baptism of Frederick Henry Schaumann, Evangelical St. Marcus Church by Rev Geo. W. Wall, Pastor.

10 Dec 1866 (21) Certification of Birth of Henry Schaumann, St. Louis. State of Missouri, County & City of St. Louis. This is to certify that Frederick Henry Schaumann, born on the twenty first day of November A.D. 1863, son of Henry Schaumann and of his wife Margarethe Dorothy Schaumann nee Ficke, was baptized by me on the ninth day of December A.D. 1866, in the presence of Sophia Rauch nee Ficke, & Caroline Huettenrauch, and in absence of the sponsors, Henry Rauch, and Frederick Meier. Given under my hand and seal of the Evangelical St. Marcus Church at the city of St. Louis, Missouri, this tenth day of December A.D. 1866. /s/ Geo. W. Wall, Pastor

15 Dec. 1866 (21) Record of Birth and Baptism. State of Missouri, County of St. Louis. I the undersigned Recorder of Deeds in and for said County of St. Louis do hereby certify that the foregoing document of writing was filed for Record in my office Dec 15 1866 & is hereby recorded in Birth Book No. 1. Witness my hand and official Seal of office this 15 day of Dec 1866 /s/ Julius Courad

18 Dec 1866 (19) Petition for Guardianship of Henry Schaumann. State of Missouri, County of St. Louis. At a term of the Probate Court of the County of St. Louis, begun and held at the City of St. Louis, in said County of St. Louis, State of Missouri, on the First Monday of December, being the Third day of December A.D. 1866, are present Hon. Nathaniel McDonald, Judge of said Court, A.S. Lindsey, Clerk, and James Coff, Marshal of the County of St. Louis: Court adjourned from day to day until the 18th day of December A.D. 1866, when the following proceedings were had: Guardianship of Frederick Henry Schaumann Guardian appointed. On motion of Margarethe Schaumann, the Court appointed her guardian of the person and Estate of Frederick Henry Schaumann, a minor aged three years, she giving bond in $100, which bond is by the Court approved and ordered

filed. Furnished by certified copy: State of Missouri. County of St. Louis. I, A.S. Lindsey, Clerk of the Probate Court of the County of St. Louis do certify that the foregoing is a true copy of the record of the appointment of Margarethe Schaumann as guardian of Frederick Henry Schaumann, as the same appears of record in my office. /s/ & dated 24 Dec 1866

18 Dec 1866 (20) Declaration of Guardianship. State of Missouri. County of St. Louis. On this 18th day of December A.D. 1866 personally appeared before me, Clerk of the Probate Court in and for said county, Margarethe D. Schaumann a resident of the county of St. Louis in the State of Missouri, aged 31 years, who being by me first duly sworn according to law, doth on oath make the following declaration as guardian of the minor child of Henry Schaumann deceased, in order to obtain the benefits of the provision made by the Act of Congress, approved July 14, 1862, granting pension to minor children under 16 years of age, of deceased officers and soldiers: that she is the guardian of Frederick Henry Schaumann born on the 21st day of November 1863 (that he is the only living child of said Henry Schaumann) whose father Henry Schaumann was a Private in company A, commanded by Captain Laux in the 2d regiment of Mo: Artilly volunteers, in the war of 1861, and that the said Henry Schaumann died at St. Louis in the State of Mo. on the 23d day of August 1866 in consequence of "Disease. He had received a pension: Certificate No. 16,459-which was surrendered to the Pension agent at St. Louis on the 8th Oct 1866"-contracted in the service of the United States, and in the line of his duty. That the mother of the child aforesaid has not remarried, and that the date of the birth of the said child is correctly stated above. She further declares that the parents of said ward were married at the county of St. Louis in the State of Mo. on the 12th day of Jany 1863, by a Justice of the Peace (see Certificate). And she further declares that his said ward is not in the receipt of any pension under this or any other act, and that neither he nor his said ward has in any manner been engaged in this rebellion, or aided or abetted the same. And I constitute and appoint Albert Sigel, Special Agent of the State of

Missouri, to present this application for pension, manage the same for me and in my name, and when a pension is granted, to receive the certificate therefor. My Post Office address is No. 1259 South 3d St. in the county of St. Louis and State of Mo. Given under my hand and seal, this 18th day of December 1866 /s/ Margaretha D. Schaumann. Also at the same time and place before me personally appeared Heinrich Rauch and John Obertin residents of the county of St. Louis in the State of Missouri, persons whom I certify to be respectable and entitled to credit, and who being by me duly sworn according to law, say that they were present and saw Margarethe D. Schaumann sign her name to the foregoing declaration and power of attorney, and that they know her to be the guardian of Henry Schaumann and that they have no interest in the prosecution of this claim. /s/ Heinrich Rauch /s/ John Obertin. Duly witnessed by the Clerk of the Probate Court, St. Louis, and filed as Declaration of Guardian for Pension for Friedrich Henry Schaumann child of Henry Schaumann, deceased. Filed by Albert Sigel, Special Agent of the State of Missouri, St. Louis.

The above documents legally established Henry as the son of the Civil War veteran Henry Schaumann, and his mother Margarethe as his legal guardian. Meanwhile, the following records (documents 24-27) suggest that Margarethe's application was accepted and was beginning to move through the examination and approval process. Had she or Henry not been qualified under existing law, the application would have been stopped at this point.

18

Application for Minor Pension

31 Dec 1866 Application for minor pension filed.

30 Jan 1867 (24) Department of the Interior Pension Office, To: Adjutant General Jany 30, 1867. Sir: You are respectfully requested to furnish official evidence of the enrollment, muster, service, duty, and cause of death of Henry Schaumann, who was a Priv in Co A, 2d Regiment of Mo Arty Vols, reported died Aug 23, 1866. If the above name is not found on the Rolls of said company, will you so state, and report as to enrollment, etc., in the case of any man bearing a similar name whom you have good reason for believing to be the soldier inquired for. When the Rolls show him to have been a Prisoner of War, let that fact be reported. No. 139,741. Respectfully yours /s/ Joseph H. Barnett, Commissioner

30 Jan 1867 (25) Department of the Interior Pension Office, To: [?] Surgeon General's Office Jany 30, 1867. Sir: You are respectfully requested to furnish official evidence of the date and cause of death of Henry Schaumann, who was a Prvt in Co. A, 2 Regiment of Mo Art Volunteers, who is reported to have died at [no entry] on the 23rd day of Aug, 1866. Please attach this Circular to your report, and return the same to this office. No. 139,741. Respectfully, /s/ Joseph H. Barnett, Commissioner

31 Jan 1867 (26) Response: Adjutant General's Office, Washington, D.C. Jany 31, 1867. Sir; I have the honor to acknowledge the receipt from your Office of application for Pension No. 139,741, and to return it herewith, with such

information as is furnished by the files of this Office. The name of Henry Schaumann is not borne on rolls of Co A 2nd Mo. Arty on file in this office. Please furnish name of Capt commanding. /s/ Assistant Adjutant General Signature *Note: The first indication of trouble. The pension file already contained previous documentation of Henry's unit, yet the A.G.'s office had no record. Below, the Adjutant General has referred the inquiry to the Surgeon General.*

13 Feb 1867 (27) Surgeon General's Office, Record and Pension Bureau, Feby 13, 1867. Respectfully referred to the Adjutant General State of Missouri for any information he may possess in regrd to the date place and cause of death of within named soldier. No record of his death now on file in this Office. These papers to be returned to this Office with report. By order of the Surgeon General /s/ signature for file 139,741

5 Mar 1867 (27) Headquarters, State of Missouri A.G. Office, Jefferson City. Respectfully returned. The name of Henry Schuermann [*sic*] does not appear on the records of the 2d Mo Artillery on file in this office. The name of William Schuermann appears on the rolls of Co F, 2 Mo Artillery. He was mustered out of service with his company Aug 25, 1865. The whole regiment was mustered out during the year 1865. /s/ Samuel P. Simpson, Adjutant Genrl. *Note: Here, the Schaumann name is misspelled in two instances. We see this problem compounded later on in the file. The pension examiners are concerned at this point with establishing Henry Schaumann's service record and date and cause of death. According to historical documentation of the Civil War, Henry Schuermann (named above) did serve in the Union Army but in Batteries E, K, and D of the 2nd Lt. Arty, the same regimental unit as Henry Schaumann but different companies. William Schuermann was also in the 2nd Lt. Arty, but in Company F (as indicated above in the response of the State A.G. Office. Henry Schaumann was the only Schaumann to serve in Company A of the 2nd Light Artillery.*

6 Apr 1867 Margarethe marries Martin Zinner in St. Louis. See 25 Mar 1868 copy.

4 Nov 1867 (30) Marriage certificate of Margarethe D. Schaumann and Martin Zinner filed, St. Louis Recorder of Deeds.

13 Nov 1867 Date of death for Henry Schumann [sic] given on 1883 certification of burial. *See 13 July 1883. Note: This apparently mistaken date of death was a problem because it alleges a date of death after Margarethe's marriage to Martin Zinner, therefore making null her claim as widow of Henry Schaumann.*

25 Mar 1868 (30) Certification of Marriage. State of Missouri, I the undersigned do hereby certify, that I united in the holy bonds of matrimony Martin Zinner, 33 years of age of the City of St. Louis, Mo. and Margarethe D. Schlaumann [sic], 31 years of age, of the same place, on the 6th day of April A.D. 1867. Given under my hand this 6th day of April A.D. 1867. Witness Friederik Salzetder, Henry Rauch, Charles Pick, Justice of the Peace, filed on Record November 4 1867 /s/ Julius Courad, Recorder

State of Missouri, County of St. Louis, I the undersigned Recorder of Deeds, County of St. Louis in and for said County of St. Louis, do hereby certify, that the foregoing is a true copy of the marriage certificate of Martin Zinner & Margaretha D. Schlaumann [sic] as of the date of filing & recording thereof as far as the same remaining Record in my office in Marriage Record Book No. 13, page 73. Witness my hand & official Seal of Office this 25th day of March 1868 /s/Julius Courad, Recorder *Note: the reason for forwarding this information to the pension board is not clear. Perhaps it was required as a matter of regulation or advised by the Zinners' attorney. Margarethe is no longer a widow; however, this would not affect young Henry's pension eligibility as a minor dependent under age 16.*

8 Dec 1868 Louise Zinner born in St. Louis.

In the 1870 US Census, 3rd Ward, 7th Subdivision, St. Louis, Margarethe, Henry, and Louise Zimmer [sic] are living with Henry and Sophia Rauch. Margarethe is working as a seamstress. This suggests that Martin Zinner was killed between Apr 1868, the estimated date of the conception of his daughter Louise, and 1 June 1870, the date of enumeration of the 1870 census. He died as the result of a teamster accident. In 1871 Margarethe married Andreas Edelmann in St. Louis.

19

Mistaken Identity

The following documents constitute the summary of pension application, subsequent audit, and rejection of claim. The claim was rejected under Section 6, Act of July 14, 1864 [*sic*], but no specific reason was recorded on the document. Margarethe could not prove at this time that Henry died as a result of a war-related cause. The claim appears to have been reopened at a later date.

22 Oct 1872 (32) Summary Brief and Rejection of Pension Application. Rejection of Original Pension for Minor Children. Frederick Henry Schaumann, Child of Henry Schaumann, Private Co A, 2nd Regiment, Mo. Arty Vols. Residence of guardian, St. Louis County, and State of Missouri. Post Office, No. 1259 South 3rd Street, St. Louis, Missouri. Attorney Albert Sigel, St. Louis, Missouri. No Fee. No contract and no material evidence filed since July 8, 1870. Frederick Henry born 21 Nov. 1863, age Sixteen 20 Nov. 1879, Margaret D. Schaumann, Guardian *Note: all preprinted language regarding amounts of pension, etc., was crossed out on this document.* Rejected Oct. 22, 1872 /s/ L. E. Dickey, Examiner; Approved as to audit November 2, 1872 /s/M.S.R. Actg., Reviewer. *Note: The following is a summary of evidence presented in the case:* Dates shown by papers. Enlistment, 14 October, 1861; Muster into rank, date-not-given; Discharge, 24 October, 1862; Death, 23 August, 1866; Invalid app. filed 24 February, 1863; Invalid pension paid to 23 August, 1866; Widow's app. filed, None; Widow paid to None; Minor's app. filed, 31 Dec, 1866; Guardian appointed, 18 Dec 1866; Claim completed [no entry]; Former marriage, none; Death

of former wife, none; Last marriage, 12 Janry, 1863; remarriage of widow, 6 April, 1867; Cause of Death, Not stated; Place of Death, Died at home. Proof as to Service: The Adjutant General USA reports name on rolls as Henry Schaumann, also the rank, company, and regiment, and the dates of enrollment as stated on preceding page. Proof as to Death: (1) Report of Adjutant General, Discharged Nov. 24 1864 [sic] at Rolla, Mo; (2) Report of Surgeon General, No information in this case; (3) Certificate of Disability, Discharged because of Femoral Hernia of right side received accidentally by falling into a ditch. Disability one-half; (4) Testimony of Army Surgeon, none; (5) Testimony of Officers, Lieut Troll certifies that injury from which the soldier was discharged was received in the service and in the line of duty; (6) Testimony of Fellow Soldiers, none; (7) Testimony of Attending Physician, Dr [Colegrove], Exam. Surg. Reported in Dec 1862 Disability one-half. Femoral Hernia of the right side, occasioned by a fall Oct 1, 1862. No evidence of date and cause of death on file in this case. Invalid pension of $4 per month granted Hernia of right side. Incidental Matter: Rejected under section 6, Act of July 14, 1864 [sic]. Attry notified. Allegations of guardian: Loyalty of Guardian, Declared; Loyalty of Wards, Declared. Summary of Proof: Guardianship, Letters filed; Other minors, None alleged; No former marriage shown; no death of former wife shown; last marriage, the marriage of Henry Schaumann to Dorothea M. Ewe nee Fike [sic] January 12, 1863 is shown by record evidence; remarriage of widow April 6th 1867 shown by record evidence; dates of birth of wards, shown by testimonial record; custody of children by former marriage, none.

22 Oct 1872 (32) Posting of Pension Rejection. Pension Office. Margaret D. Schaumann, St. Louis, Guardian, minor Henry Schaumann Priv. A, 2d Mo. Art. Died at home Aug 23, 1866. Respectfully referred to the Adjutant General, for official evidence of service and death. /s/ Joseph H. Barnett, Commissioner [illegible line]. Received, Dec 31, 1866, Albert Sigel, St. Louis, Mo., Attorney. [Notes]: pension [?] 137868. Letter from medical testimony showing cause & date of death 1868 [when received]. Attorney

contacted Jany 11, 1870. Rejected under Sec 6, Act of July 4, 1866. Posted Oct 22, 1872. Atty so informed. *Note: The pension number on this document does not match previous file numbers. Citation of an Act of July 4, 1866, on which this rejection is based, probably meant to refer to the Act of July 14, 1862. There was no Act of July 4, 1866.*

13 Jul 1883 (33) Certification of Burial Certificate. St. Louis. Name of Deceased Henry Schumann [*sic*], Age 36, male, white, occupation [no entry], place of birth Germany, length of residence in St. Louis [no entry], place of death Victor Street, exact locality [no entry], date of death November 13, 1867, cause of death Tuberculosis Pulm. I certify that I attended the person above named [no entry] last illness, who died of the disease stated, on the date above named. [no physician's signature]. Attending physician [no entry], place of burial Holy Ghost Cemetery, undertaker [no entry]. Office Health Department, St. Louis, Mo. July 13 1883. I certify that I have examined this certificate, and find it to accord with the record on file at this office. /s/ Clerk of Health Commissioner and Board of Health [Illegible notation on the bottom of certificate copy]. *Note: Attached to this certificate is a copy of Nomenclature of Diseases originally on the back of the above Burial Certificate. The item marked appears to be:* Class 1. Zymotic. Order 1. - Miasmatic. Fever, Puerperal. *The forms are stamped received in the US Pension Office Dec 4, 1883. Note: This document is believed to be erroneous. However, it probably contributed to the difficulties with Margarethe's pension application. The date of November 13, 1867, as the date of death of Henry Schaumann comes after the documented marriage date of Margarethe and Martin Zinner. The cause of death is listed as tuberculosis, a disease difficult to prove as a war-related cause of death. No attending physician certificate was ever produced contemporary with Henry's actual date of death in 1866. The belief that this is an inaccurate document is supported by two things: (1) the Schaumann name is misspelled as Schumann; and (2) the age at time of death is wrong. According to the age Henry gave at the time of his enlistment in 1861, age 37, he would have been age 43 in 1867, not age 36 as the Burial Certificate says. There was a Henry*

(Heinr.) Schumann–a druggist, age 28, living with his wife and three children in Ward Two, St. Louis, according to the 1860 US Census. His age in 1860 corresponds with the age of the Henry Schumann who died in 1867. Furthermore, this is likely the same Henry Schumann who served as a private in the 41st Mo. Infantry, Company G, mustered in St. Louis in the fall of 1864 and garrisoned at St. Louis until July 1865 when the unit was mustered out. Although the two men lived in the same general neighborhood of St. Louis and each served in the Civil War on the Union side in units originating in St. Louis, Henry Schumann and Henry Schaumann were obviously different persons.

20

Reopening of Pension Application

In the following documents, Andreas Edelmann has taken up the cause on behalf of Margarethe, trying to prove young Henry's eligibility for back pension benefits as a minor under age 16—although Henry is by now age 20—perhaps with the intent to collect back pension pay thus far denied to both Margarethe and Henry. Edelmann has retained an attorney and managed to get the case reopened. He is clearly trying to establish the cause and date of Henry Schaumann's death. In Michael Laux's affidavit the single hernia has become a double hernia; later on, Capt. Laux offers a completely different story, possibly to reinforce military service as a direct cause of Henry's death.

Dec 1884 (34) Reopening of Pension Application. Declaration for Pension of Children under Sixteen years of age. State of Missouri, City of St. Louis. On this 6th day of December A.D. 1884 personally appeared before me the Clerk of the Circuit Court the same being a court of record within and for City and State aforesaid; personally came Andreas Edelmann a resident of St. Louis in the State of Missouri aged 48 years, who, being duly sworn according to law, makes the following declaration in order to obtain the pension provided by Acts of Congress for children under sixteen years of age: That he is the only legal guardian of Friedrich Heinrich Schaumann a legitimate child of Henry Schaumann who enlisted under the name of Henry Schaumann at St. Louis, on the 24th day of November, A.D. 1862 [sic] in the late War of the rebellion, who died during the year 1866 when the cholera was raging in St. Louis Mo. and no records of the death were kept at St.

Louis and who bore at the time of his death the rank of Private in Battery A, 2nd Mo. Arty, that he left his widow surviving, that the above named [is] the only surviving legitimate child of said Heinrich Schaumann who is under sixteen years of age at the time of his death, of whom none died, that said child was the issue of said soldier as follows, the dates of their birth being as hereinafter stated: Friedrich Heinrich, of soldier by Heinrich Schaumann, born Novbr. 21st, 1863. That the father was married under the name Henry Schaumann to Margarethe Figge [*sic*], there being no legal barrier to such marriage; that the said children have not aided or abetted the rebellion; that his residence is at No. 2316 Cerile [Cecile] street, in the City of St. Louis, State of Missouri and that his post office address is St. Louis. /s/ Andreas Edelmann. Duly witnessed by Anthony Boednicker and John D. Miller 1049 Allen Ave and 2900 S. Broadway, St. Louis, respectively *Note: Mr. Edelmann is not at this point the official guardian of Henry Schaumann. Also, on this form the name of Martin Zinner is listed as the father of Henry but is crossed out and replaced with Henry Schaumann. For the first time we see cholera listed as the probable cause of death. The enlistment date is incorrect suggesting that the confusion of names continued.*

15 Aug 1885 (35) US Pension Office: Re-Opened. War of the Rebellion Subsequent Acts. Minor's #139,741 Henry Schaumann Co A. 2nd Mo. Lt. Arty. Examiner: Please work Up /s/ BRM] Aug 15 1885, [with notation]: "act under which rejected, repealed" [illegible signature] *Note. This document contains a list of several dates and appears to be a cover document related to the traffic of Margarethe Schaumann's claim. The last date recorded is 22 Oct 1872. Across this document is stamped the words REJECTED RE-OPENED.*

27 Sep 1886 Rosina Edelmann born in St. Louis, adopted by the Edelmanns.

27 Aug 1887 (36) Fee contract between Andreas Edelmann, guardian of minor of Henry Schaumann, Company A, 2nd Reg. Mo. L.A. Volunteers, and E.H. Reeves of Washington,

D.C., agent. /s/ A. Edelmann, 2204 Gravois Ave., St. Louis, Mo. Agent's acceptance of contract. $25 due to agent if pension granted /s/ E.H. Reeves, 31 Aug 1887. *Note: This copy is not signed as approved by the Commissioner of Pensions. Under the provisions of the Pension act of 1884, these contracts allowed an agent to act on behalf of the pension claimant and were a common practice. However, under the law the allowed fee was $10. A contract for $25 like this one would have been illegal. The $10 ceiling remained in effect well into the 20th Century as an aid to veterans as late as the Vietnam era, being repealed by congress only in 1988.*

25 Nov 1887 (38) General Affidavit of A. Edelmann. State of Missouri, City of St. Louis. In the matter of minors pen. Case No 139,741 of Andreas Edelmann gdn of minor of H. Schaumann late of Co A, 2nd Regt. of Artillery Mo. vols. On this 25th day of November A.D. 1887, personally appeared before me a Justice of the Peace in and for the aforesaid City duly authorized to administer oaths, Andreas Edelmann, aged 52 years, well known to me to be reputable and entitled to credit, and who, being duly sworn, declared in relation to aforesaid case as follows: That Doctor Emil [Lumann] & J.C. [Provesenor] the only surgeons that treated the deceased Henry Schaumann are both death [sic]. His Post Office address is #2204 Gravois Road St. Louis, Mo. /s/ A. Edelmann Duly witnessed and filed as Additional Evidence No. 139,741, Andreas Edelman, Henry Schauman Late of Co. A, 2 Regt. of Mo. L.A. Filed by E.H. Reeves, Washington, D.C.

25 Nov 1887 (39) Proof of Disability Affidavit of M. Laux. State of Missouri, City of St. Louis. In the pension claim No. 139,741 of Andreas Edelman-gdn- of minors of Henry Schaumann late of Co A, 2 Regt of Mo-L.A. On this 25th day of November A.D. 1887; personally appeared before me a Justice of the Peace in and for the aforesaid city, duly authorized to administer oaths, Michael Laux, aged 64 years, whose Post Office address is No. 915 Shannudah [sic] Street, St. Louis, Mo., who being duly sworn according to law, states, that he was acquainted with Henry Schaumann, who served as a Private in Co. A, 2d Regt. of

Artillery Mo. Vols. That the said Henry Schaumann while in the line of his duty, at or near Rolla in the State of Missouri did, on or about the 20th day of October, 1862 become disabled in the following manner, viz: jumping a creek near Rolla Missouri fell back on a stump–incurred double hernia on both sides, said Henry Schaumann was discharged on surgeon Certificate of Disability at Rolla, Mo., and sent home to St. Louis, Mo. That the facts stated are personally known to the affiant by reason of being with the soldier at the time, serving as Captain of Co A, 2nd Regt. of Artillery Mo. Vols. and further by reason of personally hearing him complain as follows, viz: Affiant states that he personally saw the rupture and hernia of the desease [sic] Henry Schaumann, and that he knows the facts above stated from personal knowledge and observation and not from hearsay. Affiant further states that he has no interest in said cause and is not concerned in its prosecution. That he is not interested in the prosecution of this claim. /s/ M. Laux. Duly witnessed and filed as Additional Evidence, Proof of Disability, No. 139,741, Andreas Edelman, Henry Schaumann Late of Co A, 2 Regt. of Mo. L.A.; filed by E.H. Reeves, Washington, D.C.

21

Christian County Venue

The following affidavit was executed in Christian County, Missouri, by Andreas Edelmann while still listing an address in St. Louis. The Edelmanns traveled back and forth for a time before moving permanently to Christian County. It should be noted that the affidavit was executed in January during the winter of 1888 in Christian County but gives a St. Louis mailing address. Previous family tradition had said that the Edelmanns moved to Billings in 1884, but this document would suggest a slightly later date, or the Edelmanns continued to own a home in St. Louis concurrently with the Billings place. Rosina Edelmann, adopted daughter of Margarethe and Andreas, was adopted after September 1886, further suggesting a date closer to 1888 for the permanent move to Billings. By this time—1888— Henry is age 25, well past the pension qualification age of 16. Nevertheless, he would have been eligible for back benefits for the period from 23 August 1866—the death of his father—until he reached age 16.

12 Jan 1888 (40) Claimant's Affidavit of A. Edelmann. State of Missouri, County of Christian. In the matter of minors Pension case No. 139,741 Andreas Edelmann-gdn-of minor of Henry Schaumann late of Co. A, 2 Regt. of Mo. L.A. On this 12th day of January A.D. 1888; personally appeared before me a Notary Public in and for the aforesaid County duly authorized to administer oaths, Andreas Edelmann aged 52 years, well known to me to be reputable and entitled to credit, and who, being duly sworn, declared in relation to aforesaid case as follows: That he is the claimant, and that he is unable, after due diligence, to obtain either medical or other evidence showing the

soldier's physical condition since his discharge and return from the service—for the reason that so far as he has been able to learn all those who had personal knowledge of the facts required are dead. Post Office address is 2204 Gravois Ave. St. Louis Mo. /s/ A. Edelmann. Duly witnessed and filed as Additional Evidence No. 139,741, Andreas Edelman gdn of minor of Henry Schaumann late of Co. A, 2 Rgt of Mo. L.A.; filed by E.H. Reeves, Washington, D.C.

14 May 1888 (41) General Affidavit of Christ Piefer & John Fritzinger. State of Missouri, City of St. Louis, In the matter of minor's pen. case No 139,741 children of Henry Schaumann late of Co. A, 2 Regt. of Mo. L.A. On this 14th day of May A.D. 1888; personally appeared before me a Justice of the Peace in and for the aforesaid city duly authorized to administer oaths, Christ Piefer - aged 47 years, whose Post Office address is #2204 Gravois Ave: St. Louis, Missouri, and Johann Fritzinger, aged 57 whose Post Office address is #2214 [Gain] Street, St. Louis Mo., well known to me to be reputable and entitled to credit, and who, being duly sworn, declared in relation to aforesaid case as follows: that they have been personally acquainted with [no entry] for 25 years, and 26 years: affiants state that Henry Schauman, the legal child of Henry Schauman deseased [sic] is under care of Mr. A. Edelmann and further that the aforesaid Andreas Edelmann was married to Margarethe Schaumann in the year 1871 at St. Louis in the State of Missouri, and further that he supports the aforesaid child since he married his mother, and further that Henry Schaumann was the only child of the deseased [sic] soldier, no other children are living and that they know [?] above stated from personal knowledge and observation and not from hearsay. They further declare that they have no interest in said case and are not concerned in its prosecution. /s/ Christ Piefer /s/ John Fritzinger This affidavit was filed as additional evidence by E.H. Reeves, Washington, D.C., case 139,741 Andreas Edelman, guardian of minors; Soldier: Henry Schaumann late of Co. A, 2 Regt. of Mo, L.A. Affidavit of Christ Piefer & John Fritzinger.] *Note: 2204 Gravois Avenue was an address also given by Edelmann, suggesting he*

was possibly using Piefer's mailing address and no longer resided in St. Louis.

2 Jun 1888 (42) General Affidavit of Christ Piefer John Knittel. State of Missouri. City of St. Louis. In the matter of Minor pen. Case No. [no entry] Andreas Edelmann Guardian of Henry Schaumann. Father deceased late of Co. A, 2nd Regt. of Artillery Mo. Vols. On this 2nd day of June A.D. 1888, personally appeared before me, a Justice of the Peace in and for the aforesaid City duly authorized to administer oaths, Christ Piefer, aged 48 years, whose Post Office address is No. 2204 Gravois Ave, St. Louis Mo., and John Knitttel, aged 36, whose Post Office address is No. 2234 Missouri Ave, St. Louis, Mo., well known to me to be reputable and entitled to credit, and who, being duly sworn, declared in relation to aforesaid case as follows: That they have been personally acquainted with Andreas Edelmann for 17 years and 15 years respectively: affiants state that the soldier [?] is death [*sic*] and that the child Henry Schaumann [. . .] and further that she or he never was previously married and the child Henry Schaumann is still under care of Andreas Edelmann the guardian of the aforesaid child, and further that the aforesaid Andreas Edelmann is the legal husband of Margarethe, the minor's mother, and further states they know the facts above stated from personal knowledge and observation and not from hearsay. They further declare that they have no interest in said case and are not concerned in its prosecution. /s/ Christ Piefer /s/ John Knittel. Duly witnessed and filed as Additional Evidence in case No. 139,741, Andreas Edelman, gdn of minors of Henry Schaumann late of Co. A 2 Regt. of Mo. L.A. Affidavit of Christ Piefer & John Knittel; filed by E.H. Reeves, Washington, D.C.

22

Proving the Claim

1 Jul 1889 (45) Notarized Copy of Letter from A. Edelmann. St. Louis, Mo. July 1 1889; E.H. Reeves Esq. Dear Sir: Please inform me what evidence is required to complete my claim. Yours truly, A. Edelmann. Response from E.H. Reeves, Pension and Claims Attorney, No. 202 5th Str. S. E., Washington (no date). Dear Sir: You should now furnish the affidavit of a Surgeon, Assistant Surgeon or Hospital-Steward showing treatment in the service for [?]. But should you be unable to furnish such an affidavit then be sure to write me the reasons-remember write me the reasons. *Note: The cause of death was critical to the claim before 1890. It is not clear who furnished this and the following copies of correspondence to the Pension Office. The documents were copied at Billings, Missouri, indicating that they originated with Edelmann.*

13 Jan 1890 (45) Notarized Copy of Correspondence of E.H. Reeves [To: Edelmann]. Dear Sir: You say that you sent a transcript from the public records showing that you were duly appointed a guardian. I have not got any record of having received a transcript, and it is not on file in the Pension Office. You must now furnish the transcript as called for under date of July 3rd. Respectfully, E.H. Reeves. Followed by this letter: E.H. Reeeves Esq, [no date] The St. Louis Probate Court furnish[ed] a public transcript of their records. It was sent to your office. Yours truly, Louis Holland. *Note: Margarethe remained the guardian of record on file; thus, Edelmann lacked legal status to pursue the claim. If there was a court document appointing Edelmann as guardian, it never made it to the Pension Office.*

8 Feb 1890 (45) Certified Copies of Various Documents. Army of the United States. Certificate of disability for Discharge. Private Henry Schaumann of Captain M. Laux Company (A) of the 2d Arty-Regiment of United States was enlisted by Capt. M. Laux of the 2d Regiment of Mo. Arty at St. Louis on the 14th day of Oct 1860 [sic] to serve 3 years. He was born in Hildesheim in the State of Hannover, is 37 years of age, 5 ft 6 ½ inch. high, dark complexion, gray eyes, dark hair and by occupation when enlisted a Mechanic. Station: Fort Wyman near Rolla, Mo. Date: Oct 31, 1862. Mich. Laux, Capt, Commanding Company. I certify, that I have carefully examined the said Henry Schaumann of Captain Laux Com'y and find him incapable of performing the duties of a soldier because of Femoral Hernia of the right side received by accident in jumping in a ditch about the 22d of this month. J.B. Pondram, Ass. Surgeon. *Note: The above documents dated 1 Jul 1889, 13 Jan 1890 and 8 Feb 1890 were notarized in Christian County, Missouri, 8 Feb 1890 and filed with the Pension Office marked "minor of Henry Schaumann A, 2 Mo Arty #39741"; the number 39,741 is marked out and the note added "childs origl 139,741" This document was apparently an attempt to furnish evidence of Surgeon's treatment to prove service-related death. However, under the law after 1890, it did not matter how Henry died, his dependents were entitled to a pension as long as his service in the Civil War exceeded 90 days, which it did. The timing of the evidence is confusing. Under the Act of 1890, which required no cause of death, Henry is past age 16 eligibility to qualify under this new act. However, if cause of death could be shown to be service-related–even at this late date–Henry would collect pension arrears.*

23 Dec 1891 (46) Fee contract between Margaret Edelmann, widow of Henry Schaumann, Company A, 2nd Reg, Mo Art Volunteers, War of 1861-65, and Frederick W. Fout, St. Louis, Mo. /s/Margaret Edelmann, St. Louis, Mo. 4 May 1892 Agent's acceptance /s/ Fredk. W. Fout, St. Louis Agent's acceptance also noted on this date for a contract with Henry Schaumann. /s/ Fredk. W. Fout, St. Louis. *Note: Margarethe is trying a new lawyer. On this same date,*

Henry Schaumann—minor of Henry Schaumann, Sr.—also completed a fee contract agreement with Mr. Fout at the same time as his mother, thus the claim could be made in the name of the widow or the child. Mr. Edelmann has apparently given up his effort. Both Margarethe's and Henry's agent agreements were for $25. Neither document was signed as approved by the Commissioner of Pensions.

11 May 1892 (48) Inability Affidavit of Henry Schaumann. State of Missouri, City of St. Louis. In the matter of the Pension Claim of Henry Schaumann minor of Henry Schaumann Co A, 2d Mo. L.A. On this 11th day of May A.D. 1892, personally appeared before me, a Notary Public in and for the aforesaid County, duly authorized to administer oaths, Henry Schaumann, aged 29 years, a resident of St. Louis in the State of Missouri whose Post-office address is 3108 California Ave, well known to me to be reputable and entitled to credit, and who being duly sworn, declares in relation to aforesaid case as follows: That he is unable to comply with the requirements of the Pension Office as to Regimental Surgeons, both the surgeon and assistant surgeon for reason that they are both dead. That he is unable to prove his condition from date of discharge up to the year "date of death" by medical testimony for the reason that Dr. [Mueller] who treated him during said time is dead. He respectfully requests that the testimony furnished through commanders and others be accepted in lieu of testimony necessary to establish claim. /s/ Henry Schaumann Duly witnessed and filed South Div. No. 139,741 Additional Evidence Claim of Henry Schumann minor of Henry Schaumann Co. A, 2d Mo. Art. Vols. Filed by Fred. W. Fout, US Claim Agent, St. Louis, Mo. Stamped received 16 May 1892.

In the following statement, Capt. Laux, now age 69, offers a completely different story concerning Henry Schaumann's disability. Either Laux's memory did not serve him correctly, or this new story was an attempt to more directly connect the cause of Henry's death to a service-related illness. The erroneous burial certificate of 1883 had indicated Henry's date of death as 1867 and tuberculosis as the cause of death. Capt. Laux appears to be attempting to connect that evidence to a service-related event.

11 May 1892 (49) Proof of Origin of Disability Affidavit of Michael Laux. State of Missouri, City of St. Louis. In the matter of the Pension Claim of minors of Henry Schaumann Co A, 2d Mo. L.A. On this 11th day of May A.D. 1892, personally appeared before me, a Notary Public in and for aforesaid County, duly authorized to administer oaths, Michael Laux aged 69 years, a resident of St. Louis in the State of Missouri, who, being duly sworn, declares in relation to the aforesaid claim, as follows: That he is the identical person who served as a Capt in Co A, 2d Reg't, Mo. L.A. Vols., and knows the above soldier, who was a member of Co. A, 2d Regt Mo. L.A.; that on or about 20th day of August, 1862, while in the line of duty, at or near Rolla, State of Missouri, said soldier incurred through being exposed to a heavy rain while in camp near or at said place, and being wet and exposed to rain and wind he contracted a severe cold, which [?] by [?] settled upon his lungs as a result of said cold contracted as aforesaid. I did not see him again after his discharge from said service but remember him so afflicted as aforesaid. That the facts stated are personally known to the affiant by reason of being Capt. of same company and regiment and being personally acquainted with said Henry Schaumann at said time. Affiant further declares that he has no interest, direct or indirect in this claim. Affiant's post-office address is as follows: 915 Shanadoah [*sic*] St. St. Louis, Missouri. /s/ Michael Laux Duly witnessed and filed as Additional Evidence, South Div. 139,741. Claim of Henry Schaumann minor of Henry Schaumann Co. A, 2d Regt, Mo. Art. Vols.; filed by Fred. W. Fout, US Claim Agent, St. Louis, Mo; stamped received by the Pension Office 16 May 1892 *Note: Michael Laux lived in the same section of St. Louis as the Edelmanns.*

20 Oct 1892 (50) Fee contract between Margaret Edelmann, widow of Henry Schaumann, Private in Company A of the 2 Reg of Mo. L.A. Volunteers War of 1861-5, and Frederick W. Fout, St. Louis, Mo. /s/ Margaret Edelmann, St. Louis, Mo. 22 Oct 1892, Agent's acceptance. Fredk. W. Fout, St. Louis, Mo. *Note: Yet another fee contract. This one was apparently an agreement with the same attorney earlier contracted, possibly to replace the previous agreement of*

1891, which quite possibly could have been rejected by the Pension Office, but we have no indication of that in the pension file. The fact that these agents continued to accept Margarethe's case is an indication that her entitlement was viable even in 1892, more than 25 years after her husband's death. This form, as in previous instances, is not approved by the Pension Office.

23

Widow's Declaration for Pension

In the following document, Margarethe apparently confused the order of her marriages. She was married to Schaumann before Zinner. She also gives her marriage date to Schaumann as 1862 instead of 1863. This is evidentially the first attempt to file for a widow's pension, which should have occurred in 1866. On the other hand, by naming Zinner as her first husband and Henry second, the issue of remarriage would be solved until 1871 when she married Edelmann. This likewise appears to be an attempt to align evidence with the 1883 burial certificate (which was erroneous to begin with).

20 Oct 1892 (51) Widow's Declaration for Pension. State of Missouri, City of St. Louis. On this 20th day of Oct A.D. 1892 personally appeared before me Fred W. Fout Jr, a Notary Public within and for the City and State aforesaid Margaret Edelmann aged [no entry] years, who, being duly sworn according to law, makes the following declaration in order to obtain the Pension provided by Acts of Congress granting pension to widows: That she is the widow of Henry Schaumann who enlisted under the name of Henry Schaumann at [no entry] on the 14 day of Oct A.D. 1861 in Co A, 2 Mo. L.A. Vol in the War of 1861-5 who was discharged at Rolla Mo. Nov. 24, 1862 and who died of consumption on the 23 day of Aug A.D. 1866. Who bore at the time of his death the rank of Citizen in St. Louis, Mo. That she was married under the name of Margaret Zinner to said Henry Schaumann on the 12 day of Jan A.D. 1862 by Squire Pickert at St. Louis, Mo. There being no legal barrier to such marriage that she had not been previously married, that her husband had been previously married

but first wife died. That the following are the names and dates of birth of all his legitimate children yet surviving who were under sixteen years of age at father's death, viz: Fred'k Henry of soldier by Claimant born Nov 21, 1862 [*sic*]. That she has not abandoned the support of any one of her children, but that they are still under her care or maintenance. That she has not in any manner engaged in, or aided or abetted the rebellion of the United States that prior application has been filed on accnt. of minor under General Law #139,741. That she hereby appoints, with full power of substitution and revocation Frederick W. Fout, of St. Louis, Missouri, his successor or legal representative, her attorney to prosecute the above claim, that her residence is No 3108 California Ave and her Post Office address is St. Louis, Mo. /s/ Margarethe Edelmann, witnessed by L. Morrison & D.C. Hanson Duly witnessed and filed as Widow Claim for Pension under the Acts of July 14th, 1862 and March 3rd, 1873. Margaret Edelmann Applicant, Widow of Henry Schaumann Co A, 2d Regt, Mo Lt. Arty Vols. Filed by Frederick W. Fout, US Claims Attorney, St. Louis, Mo. *Note: Friedrich Henry Schaumann was age 29 by now. Nevertheless, subsequent documents show that Margarethe's application was placed in the application process possibly based on the new alleged cause of death furnished by Capt. Laux. This document is believed to be the first time a widow's application for pension was filed by Margarethe. She reversed the order of her marriages. She had been married before her marriage to Henry Schaumann but not to Martin Zinner. Her reference to a previous marriage by Henry Schaumann cannot be substantiated. Meanwhile, she gave the same address that her son Henry gave in St. Louis as her place of residence, although both were living in Christian County, Missouri.*

6 Apr 1893 (53) Department of the Interior Bureau of Pensions, Washington, D.C., April 6, 1893. Southern Division No. 562,905 [To: War Dept.] Henry Schaumann, Widow. Sir: It is alleged that Henry Schaumann enlisted Oct 14, 1861, and served as private in Co A, 2 Regt Mo. Art. Capt. M. Laux-Cmdg Co. and was discharged at Rolla, Mo, Nov 24, 1862. It is also alleged that while on duty at Rolla, Mo. on or about Aug 1862, he was disabled by cold resulting in

lung disease. In case of the above-named soldier the War Department is requested to furnish an official statement of the enrollment, discharge, and record of service so far as the same may be applicable to the foregoing allegation together with full medical history. Please give the rank he held at the time he is claimed to have incurred the disability alleged, and if records show that he was not in line of duty during that period, let the fact be stated. Very respectfully /s/ acting commissioner *Note: This new declaration for widow's pension was numbered 562,905.*

6 Apr 1893 (54) Request for Location Verification. Southern Division. Department of the Interior Bureau of Pensions, April 6, 1893. Respectfully requested of the Adjutant General USA a report from the records of his office as to the presence or absence, on or about August, 1862, of Michael Laux, late Captain of A, 2 Mo Art. and the station, at that date, of the Regiment. Widow Claim No. 562,905 Henry Schaumann A, 2 Mo. Art. /s/ Commissioner. [Reply:] To Record and Pension Office, War Department, Washington, Apr 7, 1893. Respectfully returned to the Commissioner of Pensions. The rolls show that Michael Laux mentioned in the preceding endorsement was present during the period named in that endorsement: Return shows him present during the period named. The station of the company and regiment was as follows [e.g.] 3, 62 Camp Hamilton near Rolla, Mo. /s/ F. Ainsworth, Colonel, US Army, Chief of Office. Document stamped received by Pension Office, 8 Apr 1893

7 Apr 1893 (55) Response to Pension Office. War Department, Record and Pension Division. Widow No. 562,905. Respectfully returned to the Commissioner of Pensions. Henry Schaumann Co A, Regt 2 Mo. L. Arty. was enrolled Oct 14, 1861 and discharged Nov 24 1862 on S.C.D. From En, 1861 to Dis. 1862 he held the rank of Private and during that period the rolls show him present except as follows: Oct. 31/62 Absent sick in Post Hospital, Rolla, Mo. Since Oct 24/62. The medical records show him treated as follows -- No record formed. By authority of the Secretary of War /s/ T.C. Ainsworth, Colonel, U.S. Army dated Apr 7, 1893 *Note: Surprisingly, this inquiry for proof of service*

netted the above accurate account; earlier responses from the Adjutant General's Office to similar inquiries in 1867 had been negative.

24

Civil War Bounty

The following document appears to be a traffic record for the Henry Schaumann Minor Claim 139,741. The last legible date on the record is 5 Mar, 1894. Across this document is stamped ABANDONED. The brief notations on this Records Jacket give some indication of the runaround the Edelmanns must have received from the Pension Office, which often requested them to provide information that was already available in the pension file while ignoring accurate records and affidavits in favor of obvious clerical and mistaken identity errors.

5 Mar 1894 (56) No. 139,741 Acts of July 14, 1862, and March 3, 1873. Andreas Edelmann #2316 Cerile Str [Cecile], St. Louis, Mo. Gdn Minors Henry Schaumann Pri. A, 2 Mo. L.A. Died at St. Louis, Mo., 1866 "Cholera" Application filed: 31 Dec 1866. Attorney: Fred W. Fout, St. Louis, Mo. [Notes]: Claimant for evidence as to origin of fatal disease. Com. off. addresses furnished. Med. cond. at dis. and continuously thereafter to death, Sept 7, 1885; Claimant one hundred days notice E.H. L.R. Aug 13/87; Recors [sic] Atty for evidence of guar., prev. mar., other marriage, of cir 472 Nov 18/87; Letter to Atty Fout same as called of Sept 7, 1885, April 30, 1892; Dec 5/93; Mar 5/94 Court Abstracts of evidence of marriage and death of soldier A, 2 Art, Mar 5, 1894; [illegible] by order of chief of div. *Note: Cholera is listed by the Pension Office as cause of death in this traffic document. Two claims, 139,741 and 562,905, were under concurrent review. On this document the date of application filing was originally entered as Dec 9, 1884, then crossed out and corrected to Dec 31, 1866, the date of the original minor's petition. The Pension office was required*

to give a 100-day notice before closing a claim file. The fact that the Pension Office used 2326 Cecile St. as Edelmann's contact address, the same address he gave in Dec. 1884, suggests that he probably never received the closure notice. He had not lived at that address for nearly a decade.

23 July 1894 $100 Civil War bounty paid to Margarethe Edelmann, Billings, Mo., widow of Henry Schaumann. Paid by the War Dept. via the US Treasury. Pension Office received notification of payment 21 Sep 1897 *See document 59.*

8 May 1896 (57) Department of the interior Bureau of Pensions. Washington, D.C., May 8, 1896. [To: Treasury Department] Sir: A claim, no. 562,905, has been filed in this office by Margaret Schaumann now Edelmann, as widow of Henry Schaumann, who was a private in Co A, 2 Reg't, Mo. L.A. Vols, and is alleged to have died August 23, 1866. Will you please to furnish with the return of this circular, a copy of such evidence as may be in your possession relative to the names and addresses of all claimants for arrears of pay and bounty, and their relationship to the soldier. Very respectfully, /s/ Wm. Lockren, Commissioner

20 May 1896 (58) Response: Treasury Department, Auditor of War Department. Washington, D.C., May 20, 1896. Respectfully returned to the Hon. Commissioner of Pensions. The records of this office show that in the case of Henry Schurman [*sic*] late private, Co D [*sic*] 2d Regiment Mo. Arty Volunteers $150 Bounty, acts of July 22/61 & July 28, 1866 were allowed to soldier (St. Louis, Mo) by Treasury Certificate No. 522638 issued April 7, 1869. Said claim was allowed on satisfactory evidence of claimant's identity. /s/ auditory Pens. Claim no. 562.905. *Note: This document again confuses Henry Schaumann, Company A, with Henry Schurman, Company D. This is possibly the same Henry Schuermann misidentified 5 Mar 1867. The following is a second attempt by the Pension Office to obtain correct payment information.*

16 Sep 1897 (59) So. Div. [S.S.S]. Exr. Department of the Interior Bureau of Pensions, Washington, D.C., Sept 16, 1897.

Respectfully returned to the Auditor for the War Department requesting a report as to whether a claim for arrears of pay and bounty has been filed on behalf of Henry Schaumann of Co A, 2 Mo. L.A. Please give the names and addresses of all claimants and their relationship to the soldier. The within report relates to Henry Schaumann of Co. D [*sic*] 2 Mo. L.A. Attention is invited to the enclosed War Department report. No other report on file. Wid. Orig. 562,905 Henry Schaumann A. 2 Mo. L.A. Very respectfully /s/ Commissioner *Note: This correspondence calls attention to the misidentification of Henry Schaumann.*

21 Sep 1897 (59) Treasury Department Second Auditor's Office. Washington, D.C., Sept 21, 1897 Respectfully returned to the Hon. Commissioner of Pensions. The records of this office show that in the case of Henry Schaumann late private, Co A, 2d Regiment Mo L.A. Volunteers $100 Bounty, act of July 22, 1861 was allowed to Margaret Edelmann widow by Treasury Certificate No 204537 issued July 23, 1894. Said claim was allowed on satisfactory evidence of Marriage and relationship of claimant to soldier. Claimant's P.O. address is Billings, Mo. No other claimant. /s/ by auditor] Claim 562,905. *Note: The pension file contains no record of this payment, other than this government document from the Treasury Department. A $100 bounty was allowed to Margarethe in 1894, 28 years after the death of her husband. There is no record that she received the payment.*

7 Apr 1900 (60). Records jacket for Claim No. 562,905. Acts of July 14, 1862, and March 3, 1873. Margaret Edelmann, 3108 Cal. Ave. St. Louis, Mo. Wid. Henry Schaumann A. 2. Mo L.A. Died at [no entry]. No other claim than Min. O. 139,741 Inv. Ctf. [Invalid Certificate] 16,459. Nov 14, 1892. Application filed: Oct 26, 1892. Attorney: F.W. Fout. P.O. St. Louis, Mo. [Notations]: Dec 5, 1893, Atty. Continuance; May 8, 1896, Atty Fout letter that declarations and record of Bureau show date of death of pensioner "Sha̲umann" as Aug 23, 1866, while death record of Sh̲umann shows death on Nov 13, 1867. Claimant's remarriage certif. shows date of re-mge April 6, 1867. Discrepancy to be explained and correct death record furnished. cir. for cause of death, [?],

151

[?] & sub. serv., divorce, [?] for list of comrades, auditor for report; Sept. 16, returned aud. report; Nov 17, 1897, Atty F.W. Fout to explain discrepancies as above [?] application, prior [illegible] death or divorce of former consorts. No divorce, physical of soldier from discharge to date of death; April 7, 1900. No action. No evidence filed since July 1897. Return to files by order chief of div. J.D. Matson. *Note: This record underscores the pension board's concerns and reasons for closing the case. The erroneous death record is cited and questions are raised concerning the date of remarriage. It says that Attorney Fout is to explain the discrepancies, but apparently he never did. This document constitutes the required 100-day notice of closure of the claim for a minor's pension. Like the Edelmann address, this notice was sent to an outdated St. Louis address on file for Margarethe's son Henry well after the family had moved to Christian County. The notice was probably never received. Across this file jacket is stamped the word ABANDONED.*

Altogether, Henry Schaumann and his survivors received Civil War pension and bounty payments totaling approximately $300, including Henry's invalid pension paid before his death, and assuming Margarethe received a widow's bounty.

Notes

Chapter 1

1. Application for Invalid Pension, 2 Feb 1863. Civil War Service Record (National Archives Publications), Roll 340 Second Light Artillery, Ru-Schm, National Archives and Records Administration, 700 Pennsylvania Avenue NW, Washington, D.C. 20408.

Chapter 2

1. The Hanover Elector became one of nine German Princes who took part in the election of the German emperor.

2. The actions of Ernest Augustus brought unrest to Hanover and prompted the famous protest of the seven University of Göttingen professors, two of whom were the Brothers Grimm who were among those summarily dismissed causing international indignation.

3. State Office of Statistics Lower Saxony, Table 12411: Population update as of December 31, 2017. A province of two million people in 1864, the population of Lower Saxony grew to approximately eight million inhabitants in 2017.

Chapter 3

1. Civil War Service Record, microfilm Roll 340, Second Light Artillery, Ru-Schm, National Archives and Records Administration, Washington, D.C. Certificate of Disability for Discharge, dated 31 Oct 1862: "He [Henry Schaumann] was born in Hildesheim in the State of Hanover." This is likely a reference to the city of Hildesheim and not the region of Hildesheim. At different times in history, both Hildesheim and Peine were the respective names of larger districts in which each city was situated. However, governing districts as such were not established in the Hanover region until 1885 by the Prussian administration. Henry Schaumann's birthdate of 1826, give or take one year because the month is unspecified in the record, is calculated from his Civil War service record, which states that on 14 October 1861 he was age 37. The St. Louis Register of Deaths listed his age at the time of death as 40 years and 4 months on August 20, 1866, which calculates to April 1826.

2. Reid, W.H., *A Concise History of the Kingdom of Hanover from the Earliest Periods, to Its restoration in 1813*. London: E. Orme, 1816.

3. Köhler, J., *Hildesheim*. Berlin: F.E. Hübsch, 1928.

4. Barnet, P., Brandt, M., and Lutz, G., Eds. *Medieval Treasures from Hildesheim*. New York: Metropolitan Museum of Art, 2012.

5. Beyse, O., *Hildesheim*. Berlin: Deutscher Kunstverlag, 1926.

6. Missouri, County Marriage, Naturalization, and Court Records, 1800-1991, St. Louis Marriage records 1860-1865, Vol. 10-11, microfilm image 464; Missouri State Archives, Jefferson City. Certified Copy of Marriage Record, State of Missouri, County of St. Louis, dated 11 Oct 1866. "Mr. Henry Schaumann, late of Klauen, near Peine, Hanover, now St. Louis Mo."

7. Completed in 1905, the Mitteland Canal did not exist in Henry Schaumann's day.

8. Müller, T., *Die Geschichte der Stadt Peine* [The History of the City of Peine]. Hanover: Madsack, 1972.

Chapter 4

1. *Chamber's Edinburgh Journal*. Vol. 5, June 13, 1846.

2. Fuer, H.B., *The Germans in America 1607-1970*, p. 33.

3. Holdcamper, F.R., *List of American-flag Merchant Vessels* (Record Groups 41 and 36), National Archives Publication 68-10, Special Lists 22, National Archives and Records Service, 1968. The Bremen Ship Ernestine was 140 ft. in length, 32 ft. 6 in. wide, with a 16 ft. hold depth. Originally put in service in 1834 as the merchant vessel Columbus, the ship was purchased by a Bremen firm in 1847 and renamed the Ernestine. It remained in Bremen service until 1864, when it was sold Norwegian. The westward passages in the Ernestine took on average 36 days.

4. Germans to America Passenger Data file, 1850-1897, Ship Ernestine, departed from Bremen, arrived in New Orleans, Louisiana, NAID identifier 1746067, National Archives at College Park, Maryland. NARA microfilm publications M259 and T905, National Archives and Records Administration, Washington, D.C.

5. Ficken, H.R., Correspondence with Ken Burchett, 19 Oct 2004, "Re: Ship Ernestine Passenger List, 19 Oct 2004. Dear Mr. Ficken, I recently saw a passenger list for the Ship Ernestine, dated 4 Jun 1850, which I understand you transcribed from the original in 2001. I believe a name on that list may be an ancestor, passenger #252 Heinrich Schumann, age 24, etc. In America the name is spelled Schaumann. My question regards one of the footnotes referring to an umlaut over the "o" in his surname. Did you mean over the "u" or was there an umalutted "o" in his name on the original list?" Ken Burchett. Reply, "Re: Ship Ernestine Passenger List. The 15 cabin passengers are not numbered on original manifest, and ISTG's formatter confused things by assigning a 2nd set of numbers (first column) and keying the footnotes to same. Thus #252 became #267, and has no umlaut (scan attached) [on file]. Given the misspellings of other known individuals, Heinrich Schumann certainly could have been a Schaumann, especially considering that Schumann is a more common spelling. Homer R. Ficken."

6. Index to Death Records in the City of St. Louis, 1850-1902. St. Louis Genealogical Society, 1999. Indexed names spelled the same or similar to

Henry Schaumann: Henry Schaumann, d. 2 May 1877, address: 1500 Chamber St.; Henry Schuemann, d. 16 Mar 1885, 1521 S. 8th St.; Henry Schuman, d. 6 Nov 1883, 4021 Texas St.; John Henry Schumann, d. 3 Nov 1875, Jefferson St., near Osage St. None of these individuals was Henry Schaumann who died in 1866.

Chapter 5

1. Stevens, W.B., *St. Louis, the Fourth City, 1764-1909.* Vols. 1 & 2. St. Louis: S.J. Clarke, 1909, 1:104. The division of ethnicity in St. Louis caused several history writers to classify the city as strongly proslavery before the war. Stevens concluded that this did not necessarily mean that St. Louis favored secession.

2. Lynch, W.O., "The Influence of Population Movements on Missouri before 1861," *The Missouri Historical Review* 16 (July 1922): 513.

3. Chauvenet, S.H., "St. Louis in the Early Days of the Civil War," unpublished manuscript. Civil War Collection, 1860-1977. Missouri History Museum, no date, 1.

4. Richardson, A.D., *The Secret Service, the Field, the Dungeon, the Escape,* Hartford, Conn.: American, 1865, 159.

5. Richardson, A.D., *The Secret Service, the Field, the Dungeon, the Escape,* 159; Blum, V.C., "The Political and Military Activities of the German Element in St. Louis, 1859-1861," *Missouri Historical Review* 42 (January 1948): 103-105; Goodrich, J.W., "Gottfried Duden," *Missouri Historical Review* 75 (January 1981): 131; "Table LL. — Nativity of foreigners residing in each State and Territory," The Eighth Census 1860, under the Direction of the Secretary of the Interior, Washington: Government Printing Office, 1866, New York: Norman Ross, 1990. Richardson inexplicitly puts the number of Missourians of German origin living in Missouri in 1861 at 200,000. The 1860 US Census tabulated 88,487. Between 50,000 and 65,000 Germans lived in and around St. Louis.

6. Kirkpatrick, A.R., "Missouri on the Eve of the Civil War," *Missouri Historical Review* 55 (January 1961): 89; Blum, "The Political and Military Activities of the German Element in St. Louis, 1859-1861", 103.

7. Börnstein, H., *Memoirs of a Nobody,* translated and edited by Steven Rowan. St. Louis: Missouri Historical Society, 1997, 283; Faust, A.B., *The German Element in the United States,* Vol. 1. New York: Houghton Mifflin, 1909 1:441.

8. Moore, F., Ed., *Rebellion Record,* Vol. 1. New York: G. P. Putnam, 1861; Vol. 9. New York: D. Van Nostrand, 1866, 29.

9. Reavis, L.U., *The Life and Military Services of Gen. William Selby Harney,* St. Louis: Bryan, Brand, 1878, 349.

10. Börnstein, H., *Memoirs of a Nobody,* 262.

11. Reavis, L.U., *The Life and Military Services of Gen. William Selby Harney,* 349.

12. Ryle, W.H., *Missouri: Union or Secession,* Nashville, Tenn.: George Peabody College for Teachers, 1931, 13.

13. Dunson, "Notes on the Missouri Germans on Slavery," *Missouri Historical Review* 59 (April 1965): 365-366; Blum, "The Political and Military Activities of the German Element in St. Louis," 107.

14. Winter, WC., *Civil War in St. Louis*, St. Louis: Missouri Historical Society, 1994, 40.

15. Primm, J.N., *Lion of the Valley: St. Louis Missouri, 1764-1980*, 3d ed. St. Louis: Missouri Historical Society, [1983] 1998, 239.

16. Snead, T.L., *The Fight for Missouri, from the Election of Lincoln to the Death of Lyon.* New York: C. Scribner's Sons, 1886, 65.

17. Rosengarten, J.G., *The German Soldier*, Philadelphia: J.B. Lippincott, 1886, 95.

18. Wurthman, L.B., "Frank Blair," *Missouri Historical Review* 64 (April 1970): 272.

19. Gerteis, L.S., *Civil War St. Louis*, Lawrence, Kans.: University Press of Kansas, 2001, 97.

20. Primm, J.N., *Lion of the Valley*, 136; Faust, A.B., *The German Element in the United States*, 1:539; Richardson, A.D., *The Secret Service, the Field, the Dungeon, the Escape*, 159; Börnstein, H., *Memoirs of a Nobody*, 265-266.

Chapter 6

1. Piston, W.G., Hatcher, R., *Wilson's Creek: The Second Battle of the Civil War and the Men Who Fought It*, University of North Carolina Press, 2000.

2. Compiled service records of Volunteer Union Soldiers who served in organizations from the State of Missouri, Roll 340, Second Light Artillery, Ru-Schm. National Archives and Records Administration.

3. Battery Muster Rolls for Henry Schaumann, Pvt., "1st Batt'y A, 2 Reg't Missouri Art'y: Roll to Dec 31, 1861. Present. Enlisted Oct 14/61. St. Louis, 3 yrs. /s/ W. Sayre, copyist; Roll Jan to Feb, 1862. Present. /s/ Sayre; Roll Mar to Apr, 1862. Present. /s/ Sayre; Roll May to June, 1862. Present. /s/ Sayre; Roll July to Aug, 1862. Present. /s/ Phandon [?] copyist; Roll Sept to Oct, 1862. Absent. Absent sick in Post Hospital Rolla Mo since the 24th of Oct 1862. /s/ H.S. Mandon [?], copyist; Roll from Aug 31 to Dec 31, 1862. Discharged for disability on the 24th of Nov. 1862. To Batt'y M.O.K. /s/ H.S. Mandon, copyist; Detachment Muster-out Roll. Benton Barracks, May 24, 1863. Discharged for disability on surgeon's certificate Nov 24/62. /s/ [?] copyist." National Archives and Records Administration.

4. Dyer, F.H.A Compendium of the War of the Rebellion, (Part 3), Des Moines, Iowa: Dyer, 1908.

5. Bulletin of the School of Mines and Metallurgy, University of Missouri, Vol. 1, December, 1908.

Chapter 7

1. Certificate of Disability for Discharge, 31 Oct 1862, recorded in the Adjutant General's Office 26 Dec 1862; Proof of Disability Affidavit of M. Laux, State of Missouri, City of St. Louis 25 Nov 1887. Copies of the Disability Discharge of Henry Schaumann may be viewed in his service record and pension file, National Archives and Records Administration, Washington, D.C.

2. Certificate of Disability for Discharge, 31 Oct 1862.

3. St. Louis, Examining Surgeon's Certificate, 16 Dec 1862, Service Record. National Archives and Records Administration.

4. Civil War Soldiers Record of Henry Schaumann Pension File, National Archives and Records Administration. According to Margarethe Edelmann in

her Civil War Pension affidavit, Henry Schaumann was previously married but his first wife died.

5. Summary Brief and Admittance to Pension Claim for an Invalid Pension under Pension Act of 1862, 29 Aug 1863, Certificate No. 16,459, Service Record, National Archives and Records Administration.

6. Application for Invalid Pension, 2 Feb 1863, Service Record, National Archives and Records Administration.

7. Summary Brief and Admittance to Pension, Service Record, National Archives and Records Administration.

Chapter 8

1. 1870 US Census, City of St. Louis, Missouri, Ward 3 (Sub-division 7), 1 June 1870, M593-812, p. 69.

2. "Cholera's Riot. The Plague's Deadly Work in St. Louis Twenty-Six Years Ago," *St. Louis Sunday Post-Dispatch*, 18 Sep 1892.

3. "Dock Street Quagmire," St. Louis Genealogical Society.

4. 1866 Cholera Map, St. Louis Genealogical Society.

5. Henry Schaumann Service Record, National Archives and Records Administration.

6. St. Louis City Death Records, 1850-1908, Vol 1, p. 244, SLGS Roll 30, St. Louis Genealogical Society, 1999.

7. Miner, J., "Clinical Remarks upon Surgical Cases in the Buffalo General Hospital—Operations for the Strangulated Femoral Hernia and Fistula in Ano," *Buffalo Medical Journal*, 7 (No. 6, 1868): 208-11; Compiled service records of Volunteer Union Soldiers who served in organizations from the State of Missouri, Missouri State Archives.

8. Henry Schaumann Pension Papers, National Archives and Records Administration.

9. Oral tradition remembrance, Arthur Schaumann.

10. Holy Ghost Cemetery Archives, Eden Theological Seminary Archives, Dr. Lowell Zuck, Webster Groves, Mo. [LDS film # 1433235].

Chapter 9

1. Martyn, H., "A Missouri Confederate in the Civil War," *The Journal of Henry Martyn Cheavens, 1862-1863,* Edited by James E. Moss, *Missouri Historical Review,* 57 (October 1962): 16-52.

2. Correspondence from Dr. Lowell Zuck to Kenneth Burchett, 7 Oct 2004. "We have microfilm records from Holy Ghost of interments between 1860 and 1906 (LDS # 1433235)...In the 23 Aug 1866 list the handwritten name of "Hy Shannon" appears, #619."

3. *St. Louis City Death Records, 1850-1908.* Vol. 1, p. 244, RDSL 9, SLGS Roll 309, Mo. Archive C 10367, St. Louis Genealogical Society. "Hy Schumann [*sic*] died 20 Aug 1866, born Germany, residence street Gratiot, cause of death Cholera, white male, age 40, cemetery Holy Ghost St. Louis." Entries are in a columnar chart, handwritten. Other Schaumann names appearing on the St. Louis Death Register in subsequent years and their death dates include: August Schaumann b. Germany d. 27 Aug 1871, buried St. Peter's; Benjamin Schaumann d. 11 Jul 1876; Henry Schaumann, d 2 May 1877 (died of a gunshot wound); Lillian Schaumann d. 3 Dec 1883; Otto Schaumann d. 24

Nov 1892; Charles Schaumann d. 30 Nov 1892; William Schaumann d. 31 Jan 1897 b. Germany buried Bethania; and Daniel Schaumann d. 17 Mar 1899. Other deaths are recorded under names similar to Schaumann; e.g., Schumann and Shuman. Henry was buried under the name Shannon.

4. Holy Ghost Evangelical and Reformed Cemetery-OC-Mo. SLGS Vol. 4. StLMO, 1982, STLGSQ, Vol. 9, No. 4 (Dec. 1976), transcribed by Mabel Faatz, St. Louis Genealogical Society.

5. *Old Cemeteries St. Louis County, Mo.* Vol. 3. St. Louis Genealogical Society, 1984. Records of this cemetery may be found at Holy Ghost Church, now on Mardel Avenue. This is not the same as the Holy Ghost Cemetery at 7133 Gravois Road, also known at one time as Old Pickers.

6. *Old Cemeteries St. Louis County, Mo.* Vol. 3. St. Louis Genealogical Society, 1984.

7. Correspondence to Kenneth Burchett, 7 Oct 2004, from Dr. Lowell Zuck, Director of Eden Theological Archives, Webster Groves, Mo.

8. Correspondence to Kenneth Burchett from Archaeological Research Center of St. Louis, 29 Oct 2004.

9. Bosenbecker, R., *So, Where'd You Go to High School? Affton to Yeshiva: 200 years of St. Louis Area High Schools*, Vol. 1, St. Louis: Virginia Publishing, 2004.

10. Wicklein, E.C., "Letters from Our Readers." *St. Louis Post-Dispatch,* 4 Jul 2011.

Chapter 10

1. Death Certificate 33258, Missouri State Board of Health; Tombstone Inscription, Rose Hill Cemetery, Christian County, Missouri; International Genealogical Index, The Church of Jesus Christ of Latter-day Saints, entry for Margarethe Dorothea Ficke, batch A05173-3, FHL microfilm 537,299. Family History Library.

2. International Genealogical Index. The Church of Jesus Christ of Latter-day Saints, entry for Wilhelmine Sophie Ficke, batch A05172-9, FHL microfilm 537,046. Family History Library.

3. International Genealogical Index. The Church of Jesus Christ of Latter-day Saints, entry for Johann Friedrich Ficke, batch A24227-5, FHL microfilm 537,299. Family History Library.

4. The history of Diepholz is adapted from Stölting, H., *Geschichtliches aus der Grafschaft Diepholz [History of Diepholz County]*, Diepholz: Schröder, 1899; Dienwiebel, H., and Streich, B., *Geschichtliches Ortsverzeichnis der Grafschaften Hoya und Diepholz [Historical Location of the Counties of Hoya and Diepholz]*, 2 vols., Hildesheim: Lax, 1988-1993.

Chapter 11

1. Missouri, County Marriage, Naturalization, and Court Records, 1800-1991, St. Louis Marriage records 1856-1860 Vol 8, p. 342 image 179; Records Index 1806-1871 male, St. Louis Marriages, image 683, Missouri State Archives, Jefferson City.

2. 1860 US Census, Missouri, St Louis, 3rd Ward, St Louis City, microfilm M653, images 79-80, Washington, D.C.: National Archives and Records Administration.

3. International Genealogical Index. Deutschland Geburten und Taufen [Germany Births and Baptisms] 1558-1898. Genealogical Society of Utah, Salt Lake City.

4. New Orleans Passenger Lists, 1820-1902, 1 Jan 1859-27 Jul 1859, microfilm Series M259, Roll 47, images 410, 313, 414, National Archives and Records Administration, transcribed: "Ewe, Friedr. Age: 26, Country of Origin: Germany, Arrival Date: June 11, 1859, Final Destination: St. Louis, Port of Embarkation: New Orleans, Port of Debarkation: Bremen, Ship's Name: Olbers, Occupation: Tailor, Gender: Male; Ewe, Magarethe [sic]. Age: 24, Country of Origin: Germany, Arrival Date: June 11, 1859, Final Destination: St. Louis, Port of Embarkation: New Orleans, Port of Debarkation: Bremen, Ship's Name: Olbers."

5. 1860 US Census, Ward 3, St. Louis, Missouri. 14 June 1860. Residence #358, M653 p. 79. National Archives and Records Administration, transcription: Family #652 Frederick Ava [sic], age 27, Occupation: Tailor, Property Value: $35, Birthplace: Hannover. Margret [sic] Ava, age 24, Birthplace: Hannover. Sophia Ava, age 10/12, Birthplace: Mo. Family #653 Henry Rach [sic], age 30, Occupation: Moulder, Property Value: $300, Birthplace: Kur Hessen. Sophia Rach, age 27, Birthplace Hannover."

6. Missouri, County Marriage, Naturalization, and Court Records, 1800-1991, St. Louis Marriage records 1860-1865, Vol. 10, p. 271 image 154, Missouri State Archives.

7. Missouri, County Marriage, Naturalization, and Court Records, 1800-1991, St. Louis Marriage records 1860-1865, Vol. 10-11, image 464, Missouri State Archives.

Chapter 12

8. Certification of Birth of Henry Schaumann, St. Louis. State of Missouri, County & City of St. Louis, dated 10 Dec 1866. Civil War Service Record of Henry Schaumann, Application for Pension, National Archives and Records Administration. Rev. George W. Wall was pastor of the St. Marcus German Evangelical Congregation from 1850 to 1867.

1. Civil War Service Records of Martin Zinner. National Archives and Records Administration.

2. Civil War Service Records of Martin Zinner. National Archives and Records Administration.

3. Missouri, County Marriage, Naturalization, and Court Records, 1800-1891, Marriage Records of St. Louis and St. Louis Co., 1806-1965, Vol. 12-13 1865-1869, p. 73, image 471, Index image 433. Missouri State Archives.

4. Family Bible of Louis and Louise Eilers, possession of J. Burchett.

5. Schaumann Family Notes of Arthur and Valentine Schaumann, undated before 1979.

6. 1870 US Census, Missouri, City of St. Louis, Ward 3 (Sub-division 7), 1 June 1870, M593-812, p. 69.

7. New York Passenger Lists, 1820-1891, 5 Dec 1864-31 Jan 1864, microfilm M237, image 290, National Archives and Records Administration.

8. Probate record of Andreas Edelman, 1881, Judicial Records, Missouri Secretary of State, Missouri State Archives.

9. Missouri, County Marriage, Naturalization, and Court Records, 1800-1891, St. Louis and St. Louis Co., 1806-1965, Vol. 15, 1868-1873, p. 54, image 463; St. Louis Marriage Records Index 1871-1881 male image 100, Missouri State Archives.

10. 1880 US Census, Missouri, City of St. Louis (first enumeration), wards 13-16 (ED 100, sheet 23-ED 120, sheet 28), NARA Series T9, Roll 722; 1880 US Census, Missouri, City of St. Louis (second enumeration), Wards 13-15 (cont'd: E.D. 248, sheet 1-E.D. 295, sheet 16), NARA Series T9, Roll 732.

Chapter 13

1. Christian County Land Records; Christian County, Missouri, Personal Property Tax Index- 1879-1900.

2. Schaumann Family Notes, J. Burchett, undated.

3. Schaumann Family Notes, J. Burchett, undated.

4. Valentine Schaumann Family Notes, undated.

5. Schaumann Family Notes, J. Burchett, undated.

6. 1900 US Census, Missouri, Christian County, ED 22, Polk Twp., (north part) Billings City Ward 1, Andrew Edelmann, image 20 of 35, microfilm T623, National Archives and Records Administration.

7. 1910 US Census, Missouri, Christian County, Polk Twp., District 0043, National Archives and Records Administration.

8. Schaumann Family Notes, J. Burchett, undated.

9. *A.S. Wallace Funeral Home Records, 1926-1945, Billings, Missouri, Christian County*, Springfield, Mo.: Ozarks Genealogical Society, 1991, p. 26, Springfield Library Center.

10. Schaumann Family Notes, J. Burchett, undated.

11. This letter from Valentine Schaumann was written to Albert and Mary Reimer who held the mortgage on part of the Schaumann farm. Mary Arnold Reimer was the sister of Agnes Arnold, wife of Friedrich Henry Schaumann. The move described in the letter did not take place. Instead, Henrietta and Agnes moved in with Margaret Schaumann. Whether this letter was ever mailed to Mr. and Mrs. Reimer is unknown. It was found among the possessions of Valentine and Arthur Schaumann.

Chapter 14

1. The description of the Civil War pension system and application process is abstracted form Claudia Linares, *The Civil War Pension Law*, University of Chicago Center for Population Economics, 2001. It describes the procedures and documents required of a Civil War soldier's dependents in order to claim a pension and provides a context for the claims of the Schaumann family.

Chapter 15

1. Schaumann, Henry File: SC 16-459. National Archive Trust Fund, 709 Pennsylvania Ave NW, Washington, D.C. 20408, transcribed by K. Burchett.

Index